GRABBED

GRABBED

Poets & Writers
on Sexual Assault,
Empowerment & Healing

Edited by
RICHARD BLANCO
CARIDAD MORO
NIKKI MOUSTAKI
ELISA ALBO

With a foreword by
JOYCE MAYNARD
And an afterword by
ANITA HILL

BEACON PRESS
BOSTON

Beacon Press
Boston, Massachusetts
www.beacon.org

Beacon Press books
are published under the auspices of
the Unitarian Universalist Association of Congregations.

23 22 21 20   8 7 6 5 4 3 2 1

This book is printed on acid-free paper that meets the uncoated paper
ANSI/NISO specifications for permanence as revised in 1992.

Text design and composition by Michael Starkman and Nancy Koerner
at Wilsted & Taylor Publishing Services

Library of Congress Cataloging-in-Publication Data

Names: Blanco, Richard, editor. | Moro, Caridad, editor. | Moustaki,
    Nikki, editor. | Albo, Elisa, editor. | Maynard, Joyce, author
    of foreword. | Hill, Anita, author of afterword.
Title: Grabbed : poets and writers on sexual assault, empowerment, and
    healing / edited by Richard Blanco, Caridad Moro, Nikki Moustaki, Elisa
    Albo ; with a foreword by Joyce Maynard and an afterword by Anita Hill.
Description: Boston : Beacon Press, 2020.
Identifiers: LCCN 2020011363 (print) | LCCN 2020011364 (ebook) | ISBN
    9780807071854 (ebook) | ISBN 9780807071847 (trade paperback)
Subjects: LCSH: Women—Crimes against—Literary collections. | Women—Abuse
    of—Literary collections. | Sex crimes—Literary collections. | Psychic
    trauma—Literary collections. | American literature—Women authors. |
    American literature—21st century. | American literature—20th century.
Classification: LCC PS509.W6 (ebook) | LCC PS509.W6 G73 2020 (print) | DDC
    810.803538—dc23
LC record available at https://lccn.loc.gov/2020011363

CONTENTS

II. INSTITUTIONS

IV. HOME

Joyce Maynard

There are certain moments we've all lived through that take hold
in our shared national consciousness. The explosion of the *Chal-
lenger*, the planes crashing into the Trade Towers, an immigrant
mother holding the hand of her five-year-old as she flees the tear
gas of the border patrol. One of those moments occurred when
we heard the voice of Donald Trump, caught on tape proudly
announcing to his buddy the perks of being a powerful man as
they related to women.

"You can grab them by the pussy," he said. "You can do any-
thing."

A month after that tape was played, again and again, on
national television, our country elected that man president—as
clear an indication as a person might ask for that we had become
a nation that condoned, and maybe even (like Trump's friend on
the tape) chuckled over, violence against women.

But there is nothing funny in the stories and poems between
these covers. Each one recounts a different and unique brand of
painful experience. The element that runs through every one of
them is clear: somebody touched somebody else in a way that
represented a profound and painful violation. In one story, the
predator reached out through the telephone line, but the place
he grabbed hold of was as vulnerable as any: the author's brain.

What it tells a person, when someone touches another
somewhere without consent—whether they grab your pussy or
your butt or stick their tongue down your mouth on the way out
the door—is that one's own body is fair game for anyone who
wants to place their hands on it. That casual grab sends a power-
ful message: a person's body is there for the pleasure or amuse-
ment of the predator, for as long or as brief a time as it continues
to amuse them.

Grabbed. It's an apt description. We're speaking about a kind of heist, not only of an individual's physical being but, very possibly, of her spirit. Or his. The stories collected here—though predominantly written by women—remind us that a man, particularly a very young one, can also be the prey. But here's the thing that distinguishes sexual predation from larceny: Stolen goods can be retrieved. Stolen innocence cannot.

And once a culture accepts "grabbing the pussy" as an acceptable activity, the culture itself is in jeopardy. When we normalize pussy-grabbing, or any other kind of grabbing, we are disrespecting our own fellow human beings and our own selves. (I would say here, we are becoming animals. But I like animals too much to put it that way. We are becoming monsters.)

The stories and poems in this book seek to remind us, grabbing is not normal. These stories stand as affirmation that our bodies are precious and sacred, and that touch still means something. And its effects linger. The writers here are offering up, with their stories, the most powerful negation of that stomach-turning Trump tape. One rich, entitled, and seemingly soulless man says it's fine to grab. The authors of these stories and poems remind us, it's not. Sexual abuse takes many forms. Sometimes the violation has been repeated many times, over years even. It may have taken place only once. "Only" once. But once is enough; the reverberations have endured into the present. Whatever it was that occurred, the fact that these writers have chosen to tell their stories stands as evidence that each is a different person for the experience of having been physically, or emotionally, grabbed. Every one of these writers lost something in that moment of violation. It is not retrievable.

I know about this because I am one such person myself. Almost fifty years have passed since my own experience of being—psychically and then physically—*grabbed*, when I was eighteen years old. I want to say that I did not let that experience define or crush me. But I am a different woman than I would have been had my first experience of sexual intimacy not been one of manipulation and intimidation. That experience provided my first glimpse of the landscape of sexuality and (these words are hard to write and harder to say) in certain ways colored it forever.

In my case, I name not one but two instances of life-altering violation, separated by twenty-five years. The first one happened when I was eighteen, when a much older and very powerful man came into my life and convinced me that his needs superseded my own. After he'd discarded me, I lived for a surprisingly long time under the mistaken sense of obligation to keep his secrets, to protect him by, in effect, cutting out my own tongue. When, twenty-five years later, I finally located sufficient courage and sense of my own worth to tell the story of what had happened when I was young, I incurred a second brand of damage, possibly more painful even than the first. As a woman telling the story of an important man who sought her out as his sexual partner, I was labeled "a leech," "an exploiter," "a big mouth," and—this, in the pages of the *New York Times*—"a predator."

I am hardly alone, as a woman who—recounting the story of some form of abuse at the hands of a powerful man—finds herself the object of derision. That's how it has gone, for as long as I can remember: Every time another woman has dared to tell her story, she risked a whole new form of violence—rape in the court of public opinion. And here is a troubling phenomenon: contempt not only from men but too often from other women. Some of the harshest critics of the memoir in which I recounted my story were female writers. Misogyny is not the sole territory of men.

They may say it never really happened. Or that the woman to whom it happened must have been asking for it. They may say, of a woman who finally locates the courage to speak up, that she's looking for money, or fame, or—as they did of me—to sell books. They may just say the woman is a liar, or that she feels guilty about some sexual encounter she engaged in and seeks to rewrite history by suggesting that she didn't actually want it. "If it really happened, why did it take her so long to speak up?" goes the question, raised (invariably) by those who seek to cast doubt on the testimony of women who stand up and tell what happened to them when they were young.

Every time I hear this, I want to call out to the blandly dismissive pundit on the television screen: *Maybe she waited because she knew there would be people like you, ready and eager to call her a liar.* Maybe she waited, knowing that our world is filled with people seduced by power, money, and influence, who cannot believe that behind the steely-eyed face of the movie producer, under the well-cut business suit, behind the desk of the well-loved congressman, or the TV star, America's favorite dad, might beat the heart of an abuser.

For as long as women have been touched, toyed with, drugged, raped, or grabbed, those same women have been dismissed and humiliated if they attempted to tell what happened. This has been the experience not only of the weak but of the strong. Anita Hill was one such woman when she testified at the confirmation hearing for the Supreme Court nomination of Clarence Thomas at proceedings that came to seem like her own trial. And lest we allow ourselves to suppose those days are all behind us, we must remember that much of the same treatment was directed at Dr. Christine Blasey Ford when she offered testimony of her experience at the hands of Brett Kavanaugh. Blaming the accuser was common practice twenty years ago, and it was alive and only marginally less flagrant in the fall of 2018.

For all of this, one might have supposed that women would have learned the lesson to remain silent about their experiences of abuse. Instead, the Trump tape—and the disclosures of multiple women concerning their alleged abuse at the hands of Bill Cosby and Harvey Weinstein, followed by many stories that poured forth in the #MeToo movement (too many now to count) and the Kavanaugh hearings—unleashed a cascade of other stories. The more women spoke, the more other women were empowered to do the same. Instead of fear, the mistreatment of the women who came forward inspired outrage, and courage, and the refusal to remain silent as our grandmothers and mothers, who may well have endured their own soul-crushing experiences, may have felt required to do.

There are ninety-one stories and poems contained between the covers of this book. For every one, there are a thousand more, not yet told. For every woman—or man—who has dared to speak her truth, or his, another hundred will be inspired to do the same.

Maybe, if we tell enough of these stories, there will be none left to tell.

Caridad Moro

With this gender-inclusive anthology of poetry and prose, we, the editors, hope to address the physical and psychological act of being "grabbed" without permission, as well as the confusion, fury, and trauma such acts can cause. The #MeToo movement, the infamous *Access Hollywood* tape, the Kavanaugh Supreme Court nomination confirmation, and the depraved and hypocritical actions of celebrities, politicians, CEOs, and other powerful people have raised the voices of individuals all over the nation in allegiance and outrage for their victims and against a culture that has allowed this behavior to continue for too long.

Inspired by these events, we asked writers and poets to add to the conversation about what being "grabbed" means to them in their own experience, or in whatever incarnation the word "grabbed" inspires. What we received is powerful, heartrending work ranging in topic from sexual misconduct to racial injustice, from an unwanted caress to rape. In this collection, our authors have mined their collective experiences to reveal their most vulnerable moments, and in some cases, to reveal moments that they have long had buried or had previously been unwilling or unable to express. What results is a collection of emotional, hard-hitting pieces that speak to the aftermath of violation, whether mental, emotional, or physical. Our voices range from emerging writers to a Pulitzer Prize winner, from a freshman college student to the former US Poet Laureate and the *New York Times Magazine*'s poetry editor, from a librarian to the fifth Inaugural Poet of the United States. In the process of compiling these pieces, we wanted relevant cultural voices to weigh in on the zeitgeist of the moment and highlight the gravity of our mission: to raise the chorus of an all-too-often silent majority.

Joyce Maynard was an obvious choice for our foreword. Her work has long been concerned with the effects of sexual politics and power on the self, the community, and society at large. Her foreword reflects on her past and how that past becomes more present every day, not just for her but for all of us. For our afterword, Professor Anita Hill represents a prime example of a person who has confronted power and privilege through an experience that changed her life—and a nation. Her essay for this collection illustrates how the humanity inherent in literature can mirror the humanity that we hope to find in the law, our judicial system, our democracy, and the world at large.

The stories and poems in this collection include the end of a young girl's innocence at a neighborhood pool party; a young man confronted about his sexuality by his violent, *machista* father; a jealous playground altercation; the dark, isolated storeroom of a young man's first job; a tongue-in-cheek parody of classic literature; and confessions of secrets held for decades. The result is a kaleidoscope of voices, perspectives, and approaches to similar experiences. From engineer to educator, from memoirist to poet, we make up an interdisciplinary group that views the same topic through a variety of lenses. We vary in religion, sexual orientation, socioeconomic backgrounds, and ancestries, but we meet on common ground on this topic, as all of us have our own work—and experiences—in the pages of this book.

Grabbed is for everyone who has ever felt alone in their experience of being grabbed, violated, overlooked, and silenced. This anthology is their voice. It is their war cry. It is their plea to be heard and be seen. We want this volume to provide hope to those who have yet to harness the power of their own story. We want our reader to cry, to laugh, to feel, to move closer to catharsis with every turned page. Years in the making, the stitching together of these important narrative chronicles not only archives this newsworthy moment in time but also pays homage to the moment when our voices rose in unison to say, firmly and finally, enough.

1

STRANGERS

WHAT WE DID THIS YEAR

FREESIA MCKEE

I counted up the poems I'd written

about violence against women
though I knew the number

is ever-growing. On the bus,
a cry moved through me like water.

I remembered the male writer
who sent me a picture of a naked stranger,

Do you think she's all right? he asked,
claiming the woman posing

was our mutual friend.
I remembered when I learned a woman's body

could be used against her. I remembered relearning
what I had learned and learned.

I remembered how it felt
all the times my friends told me they thought

I hated men. If I was honest,
I would have told you there were women I hated.

I wanted to be right and I wanted to be wrong.
I was no longer surprised when I didn't feel anything.

I wanted to stop writing.
The man's hairy

arm pressed up against me
on the bus

as he slept and I read an account and I read another.
I took a drink of water and I took another.

Some men lost their jobs, but not their investments.
Some people said *I'm ready to listen*.

How unready was I to hear it, wondering
where we'd been for each other every day of our lives.

THE TRUTH IS
I NEVER LEFT YOU

ALEXANDRA LYTTON REGALADO

What's your name? the man in the airplane asked again. *Violetta,*
I said. I was seven years old, and my mother and grandmother
were sitting one row ahead, each one holding a twin on her lap,
and my little brother was whining in the window seat. There was
no more room, and so I had to sit alone. The man gave me a
grandfatherly smile and offered me his window seat.

I didn't like my name. Violetta wasn't a proud bloom like the
sunflower that shot straight up and turned its wide face to stare at
the sun; Violetta was a shy flower that crouched in the shadowy
corners of the garden. Violetta had furry leaves and flowers
with bowed heads. Violetta, the color of a bruise, I thought, not
Violetta, the color of royal robes.

The man leaned in close and touched my arm. *Antonietta?*
I shook my head, said my name again, louder. *Ah, Violetta, what
a beautiful name.* As the plane took off, I pressed my face to the
window, imagining the trees closing in, vines tightening around
the jungle, a temple-memory I'd invented full of macaws, jaguars,
and Mayan secrets etched in stone. It was more likely there
were *guerrilleros* camped out in the foothills; we were leaving
behind soldier-sentineled, sandbagged corners of the city, daily
bombings of transformers and power outages, dusk-to-dawn
curfews. It was 1980, and the civil war had begun in earnest. We
were relocating to Miami, where my father, a new house, and a
new school waited for us. I'd spent my last days in San Salvador
at my grandmother's house, carving my initials into walls, palm
trunks, the undersides of tables in the hopes of finding them
when I returned.

In those days, the plane wasn't filled with passengers carting oil-soaked boxes of Pollo Campero or string-tied boxes of Lido cakes; blue-eyed, Bible-toting missionaries; women from the countryside wearing their city best topped with ruffled and ribboned kitchen aprons; businessmen; families headed to Disney; women darting out for a shopping getaway; men in straw sombreros who eat trays of food with their fingers, who wrap the bread and butter in napkins to save for later, who bashfully ask you to fill out their immigration forms, which they carefully sign with an X. These are the SAL-MIA passengers of 2017. I suppose then, in the El Salvador of the early '80s, the plane was filled with people fleeing, and no matter how much it hurt to leave, at least my family and I were leaving by choice. The war had erupted around us, but we were intact; other families had broken in its grip.

I wasn't aware of any of those things when I was a seven-year-old girl, but I suppose my mother and grandmother were torn between relief and guilt: we were going to be safe, but for all of those left behind, the war was just beginning. That day, they had a lot on their hands: two squirming infants and my four-year-old brother, who cried the whole way and probably had an ear infection. I don't remember the first part of the flight; I might have slept. I snapped to when my brother was yelling, banging his head onto the seat, shaking my tray table open and startling me.

Beside me, the man was taking the last sips of his drink and swirling the glass; I distinctly remember the two ice cubes running circles along the base of the glass, one chasing and one fleeing. He clapped his hand on my leg and leaned in to whisper, *Buenos días, bella durmiente*. His breath was heavy with whiskey—a smell that even today feels like a chloroform-soaked handkerchief—and though I couldn't explain it then, I could see his eyes had gone sleepy, that his words fell out of his lips like tangled yarn; he was drunk. And I was a deer in the woods. Flickering ears, coat twitching, little front hoof raised, ready to dash into the thicket. But his tray, with picked-over food and balled up napkins, created a barrier.

I poked my mom's shoulder through the gap in the seats, pressed my face into the crack, and called, *Mami, Mami*. One of the twins had kicked over a drink, and she was trying to mop it up—the cranberry stain on the crotch of my brother's pants would never come off. The man put his hand on the tray's edge and along the cleave of my armpit, and I felt the heat like a stove I should back away from. *Mami, Mami*, I called, and she turned and angrily said, *¡No puedo! ¡Ahorita no!* I started crying, quietly at first, turning toward the window, and the man began to rub my back in broad strokes. Violetta, the rag doll. Violetta, crushed underfoot. Violetta, dress the color of crumpled petals.

The sobs rattled through me, and the man brought his puffy-eyed face close to mine, asking what was wrong. I tucked my hands beneath my thighs, leaned forward, tried to make myself into a ball. He talked into my ear, saying things you would say to a testy pony. He complimented my dress, smoothed the sleeves, pressing down on my shoulders. His hands were layering me with something heavy, like wet sand, something dark and suffocating. It was hard to tell where the wrongness originated; it spread all over us, tangled and confused. He touched my cheek. *Is it because you're sad you're leaving?* I shrugged his hand off and wiped my face. Then I shook my head yes, took a breath, and sat back. It was a good way out, if I wanted to be polite—and I did. But he reached for my hand and started singing, *Don't cry for me, Argentina . . .* the whole song worming into my ear.

How no one noticed, I will never know. The stewardesses were probably at the front of the plane picking up trays, the other passengers across the aisle minding their own business, and maybe we appeared to be a crying girl and a consoling grandfather. But his voice in my ear sounded like a ghost mourning his own funeral. *Don't cry for me*, the man sang. And I knew this man was no one's grandfather.

Violetta, plume of smoke. Violetta, the hottest blue-black of the flame. Violetta, flying over the sky's last light. I tried to unlock my hand from his, asked him to please let me out. The man suddenly threw my hand down and curtly said that his back hurt. *Could I please just climb over?* He clicked his table closed and put the tray aside. And because this was my escape, I did what I had to. I lifted my leg over the hurdle of his lap. His hands were resting on his knees, and as I stepped over, I felt him grab me between my legs. Seconds passed, and I was stuck with my leg in the air, above the dam he had built, the ridge of his fingers pressing against my underwear. The man leaned back, eyes closed but with a slight smile. I grabbed onto the back of my mother's chair, hopped, and pulled myself away from him. I felt as if I had snapped out of a husk and fallen into midair.

I cried in the aisle, red-faced, next to my grandmother, and tried to crawl over to my mother, who was already wrung dry from my siblings' push and pull. I wanted to figure it out on my own because even then I knew she was taking on too much. I felt ashamed because I felt implicated somehow. What had happened to my body was so precise, and yet I couldn't make sense of it. The only thing I could offer was a kind of surrender. My mother had been right, I'd been frivolous because I wanted to wear a stiff-starched party dress; I should've known better. The man had seen my weakness. His hands were crushing, heavy weights. How could I explain it to my mother? Probably she assumed I was letting myself be carried away, and she just looked at me as she bounced my sister, who was also crying. *Ya, ya, ya, vaya, vaya—* surely it was all that she could muster, the soft shushing sounds you make to a colicky baby in the middle of the night. I know she was torn, taking her children to live in safety, in a country that offered a full spectrum of opportunities, but leaving behind family, sisters, friends, and her country, which was tearing itself apart from the inside, split in two as if by an earthquake.

I also felt pulled in different directions—to stay quiet, to say what had happened. I just cried and cried, holding my skirt down with both hands, covering the place my grandmother had reminded me always to wash for fear of a mushroom growing. And my mother asked again and again, *What happened? What happened?* And I could only glance back toward the man, the man who pretended to sleep, his eyes closed, his mouth open, even emitting a soft snore. His song looped in my brain: *Don't cry for me, Argentina.* I cried harder as anger ripped through me.

Years later I asked my mother about the incident on the airplane, and she claimed not to remember, even insisted I'd made it up. Maybe I was exaggerating, she said—it was probably a pesky old man who was trying to make me laugh. Sometimes, when I remember the scene, she understands what I'm trying to communicate with my eyes, yells at the man, and holds me in her lap the rest of the way. And honestly, I can't remember what happened. Did I go back to my seat? Did anyone say anything?

What I do know: that moment on the airplane was the first time I doubted myself. What had really happened, just minutes ago? Had I imagined it? Was it possible to confuse a touch to my very own body, to my most private center? It seemed to me that not long ago, I had inhabited my mother's body, had been fed from her body, slept in her arms. And yet, as I stood in that airplane aisle, I was split open, disconnected. I was my own separate being, suspended above the clouds, and also speeding to some unknown somewhere. Mid-flight, traveling between two worlds, I had to stake a claim on my body and say, this is mine, this flesh and blood, my mortal and beating heart, alone or accompanied, regardless of who came before me and who will come after me. I felt the weight of my bones and knew: no matter the coordinates of the ground I'm standing upon, this is me, Violetta.

SWEET SIXTEEN

BRENDA CÁRDENAS

Sweet sixteen in patched Levi jeans
and spaghetti strap tees, we walked
a mile to meet the bad boys kicking back
at the park, Newports nearly tumbling
from their bottom lips as they flicked
wheels to flint and waited for a spark.

We strolled in with six-packs
of Pabst and sass, asking for a joint
and a motorcycle ride, secretly wishing
for a date to the carnival or concert
or next beer bash. But we barely popped
the tops of our cans, had any chance
to joke or flirt or speak of summer plans
before dusk deepened to dark, before

he pressed me against tree bark, tightened
his vise of a body to mine, and grew
ten hands that grabbed everywhere,
even the hair at the back of my head to stop
my thrashing neck. By some dumb luck,
he could not trap my ten-alarm screech,
its siren rupturing his will.

Still, I often wake straining and mute,
knowing either he or the tree will swallow
me if I cannot scream. And what of her?
The one who breezed into the park with me
that summer eve, all cherry lip gloss
and glitter eyes, all cool façade melting
on the inside, all sweet sixteen
with her firefly heart waiting to spark.

SHE SAID STOP HERE

CYNTHIA WHITE

and then Jen showed me the spot
where the man with the knife
might have killed her and
now she comes to visit because
she says a place like this needs regular care.
There ought to have been a crouching beast
of a monument. Or snake pits. Or Dante's river
of fire and blood. But it was an everyday
kind of spot. Sunning itself by the roadside,
it continued placid, mute as the dirt next door.
Jen had brought a picnic. We drank lemonade.

FOUND POEM: CHORUS TO A GIRL

HOLLY MITCHELL

Are you a waitress? You belong in an office. You stupid bitch
beautiful you are a princess you need help with that. I love you
mama baby sexy. Can I grab you a bottle? I have money I like
horsey I like how you walk. Drink with me. Daddy don't bite
unless you want big tips. They're yours for a neck for you three
pennies in the dirt. Dyke I like how you know we mean you.
Faggot was I supposed to know from behind? You don't know
what's down there man. Nothing but flies. He she it sir miss.
Woman should smell like woman. Little dead can you solve this
problem? Don't look so real. Cut your tongue or I will. Clean it
in whiskey.

FLASHBULB MEMORY

IRIS JAMAHL DUNKLE

*A flashbulb memory is a detailed and vivid memory that
is stored on one occasion and retained for a lifetime. . . .
They demonstrate that the emotional content of an event
can greatly enhance the strength of the memory formed.*

—DANIEL SCHACTER, *Searching for Memory:
The Brain, the Mind, and the Past*

Where were you when it happened? A bathroom
stall. White tile floor. Fluorescent lights that blinked.
What happened before? Bought button candy
at Hickory Farms. My mom let me walk
around the mall on my own. First time. I
was ten or eleven. Can you describe
the events as they occurred? I was peeing
on the toilet, pants down around my ankles,
when a man crawled under the wall
between stalls. Stood up. Hair wild.
He wore oversized tube socks with red stripes.
After, I walked out of the public restroom,
down the long hall, and emerged
as a ghost in the crowd. I tried to swallow
everything that had happened like giant stones.
Speaking the words would let them fly out, make
them real. When I met up with my mom in
JC Penney's I didn't say a word, tried to remain a ghost.
Of course, there were police, and mug shots and
a nice detective who came to our home.
But first there was the shame. The animal
noise I'd made, I'm still making, years later.

KIDNAPPED GIRLS

CATHERINE GONICK

One is not born, but rather becomes, a woman.

—SIMONE DE BEAUVOIR,
The Second Sex

Yeah, but some things we seem almost born knowing, don't we?
Like our knowing to follow those first-grade Oakland boys
who knew to take us, their girl classmates and neighbors,
straight up our hilly block to an abandoned shack
in an empty field. The shack was just across the street
from one boy's house, where a mother was at home,
but still seemed far away and kind of dangerous
once they got us in there. Those boys also knew to order us
to take down our pants, and we knew to comply and act
like prisoners though we knew this wasn't really real—
nobody made a fist or even touched us—which made me feel
a little silly. Then the boys ran out of ideas, got bored,
and our whole gang drifted away.

Things were different when my grandmother was visiting.
On another kidnapping afternoon, who knows how, she knew
to suddenly loom, huge and backlit, at the head of an alley
two doors from my house. We girls had been abducted
only moments ago, and the boys were busy showing us
theirs if we showed them ours. Everything seemed okay until
the dark figure that was Grandma started cawing
like a giant crow as she bawled us out and everyone ran.
Where is she now that she's needed, in Oakland and everywhere
slavers have grown into their knowing?

They're getting away with it, Grandma, but I'd like to think
this nonsense never could have happened on your watch. O my stern
Grandma, who stood so firmly against any illegal, impure,
and dangerous forms of sex (you knew all sex was dangerous
to women), how I would rejoice to hear you caw again,
your voice gathering power like an unbearable siren
heard by everyone on Earth, until it could finally disperse
all bad boys grown old, from girls who can no longer escape.

HITCHHIKER

CYNTHIA WHITE

After Charles Rafferty

The tail lights of a Pontiac
burned by the roadside, the air
around me pearly with fog.
Like a vagabond princess,
I leaned back against green plush,
told the man where to drop me.
The scars have paled with the years
but sometimes I wake to the snick
of a spring-blade knife. I've kept
my silver anklet and patched up shirt,
a five line story I tore from the paper,
naming me "unknown." It's all
still there in a bottom drawer,
relics of another life, but also proof
that I'm alive,
that I met what came my way.

TUESDAYS

YVONNE CASSIDY

That first Tuesday you almost don't go. You can find plenty of excuses. It's January. It's dark already and raining. You want to watch Obama being inaugurated on telly. And anyway, you don't need to go. There is nothing wrong with you. You feel fine.

Your therapist says that *fine* isn't a feeling, that it stands for *Fucked-Up, Insecure, Neurotic,* and *Emotional.* It makes you laugh when she says this. You've been seeing your therapist for 15 months and you don't know what you'd do without her. She's worth the €100 a week, €200 on the bad weeks. That first Tuesday, you only go for her, because you told her you would.

You never knew this place was here, right off Merrion Square. The entrance is next to the office building where your friend works, and even though you know she'll be long gone, you pull your hood tighter around your face. In the seconds between ringing the bell and the door being buzzed open, you almost turn around and leave but then it is open and there's the woman at reception who you recognize from the intake assessment. You go upstairs. You are early—you're always early. There's someone waiting in the waiting room. You lock yourself in the bathroom.

At two minutes to seven you come out. The door to the main room is open and you walk straight in, like it is any room. Four couches are set up around a rug and one is still empty. You take a seat. You check again that your phone is turned off.

You don't look at the others until you have to, until it starts. They're not like you, that's the thing you make up your mind about first. You have nothing in common except this thing you wish you didn't have in common. Half are men and you know you shouldn't be surprised but still you are. One is a taxi driver. One works in IT. One of the women has breast cancer. They are all older than you and from the northside, with accents that sound different than yours. You are from the southside, from an affluent area that some would call privileged. You're not a snob, you don't care about things like money or where people are from. It doesn't matter—you were raised to believe it doesn't matter—but sitting here, suddenly it does. Things like this don't happen to people like you. Money should protect you from some things.

You don't remember what was talked about that first night. You remember being afraid that the others are going to talk about the details of what happened to them, details you don't want to know. The details of what happened to you are hazy—that's part of the problem. You don't need to know theirs.

You hate the therapists straight away—that's the other thing you remember from that first Tuesday. They are both women—one black, one white—and they hardly say anything. They sit on hard plastic chairs you hadn't noticed at first. You wonder why that is, if it's because they were last in or the unwritten rule is that the victims are the ones who deserve a comfy seat. You remember the force of that thought hitting you, the snag of the word *victim*.

Did you speak that Tuesday? Probably, yes, definitely. You don't remember what you said but you know now, looking back, that you spoke because you thought you were supposed to, that you should. You are a good girl. You do what you are told. Maybe that's what got you here.

You come the next Tuesday and the one after. On Fridays, you tell your therapist how much you hate all of them, how you are not like them. You tell her this isn't necessary—it's not like you have proper memories, it's not like it affects you. This thing happened thirty years ago—some days you still wonder if it happened at all. You don't tell your therapist just how hard you cry in your car on Tuesday nights on the way home.

You keep coming. You sit and look at the rug. You listen to

the others talk about their families and the Church and one man who goes to visit someone's grave. The woman with breast cancer has started to get comfortable talking about her inner child. Fuck that. Fuck her. A new woman joins the group. It happened to her when she was in her 20s, living in New York. She goes on and on about how badly the NYPD handled it. When the white therapist asks her how she feels, she goes silent, and twists her ankle around and around, the sound of its clicking filling the room.

Memories come in shapes you don't expect. You thought memories were visual, not physical, but you start to feel them in your body, like your body is not your own. You wanted memories, but you don't anymore. Now you want your body back, not to betray you like it did before.

One Tuesday, the black therapist says something. She says that it's easier for children to think that they are bad than to believe the world is bad, that it's too scary for them to think that. You've heard this before—some version of this. But that's the first Tuesday the tears come in the room instead of in the car on the way home.

There are more of them after that. Feelings. Not "fine" anymore. The room holds it all, the tears and the rage—a teddy bear kicked once so hard that it hits the wall. Sometimes there can only be silence. Sometimes you sit cross-legged on the floor with another woman—a girl—drawing together, the only sound, crayon on paper.

You start to scream in the car on the way home, bouncing your hands off the steering wheel. You blare Alanis Morissette, 4 Non Blondes, Eminem to cover the sound, compose yourself at the traffic lights. You buy a punchbag and boxing gloves—items you've wanted for as long as you can remember—and you punch until you are sweating and breathless. You have hot baths, hot tea, hot toast and butter, you put something easy on the telly. On the nights it is really bad you sit on the bedroom floor in the corner with a blanket and your teddy bear and a coloring book, waiting for it to pass. Once, you make a mistake and schedule a client presentation for a Wednesday morning. You show up, you get through it, of course you do, you're a shower-upper. But you don't make that mistake again.

The Tuesdays pass. Spring. Summer. You always know how near or far away Tuesday is in the week without having to check. You don't look forward to it but you don't hate it either. You don't miss it except when you're on holidays. You still look down when you turn off Merrion Square, breathe easy when you are buzzed in. It's a miracle you've never run into your friend from the office next door. Sometimes there are workshops organized on Saturdays, retreats away in the country. You always go, even when it means changing your plans, even once when it's your birthday. Yoga is your cover for everything. People don't ask much about yoga.

120 Tuesdays. That's how many you go for, give or take. You miss four when you travel to New York where you meet someone you like, someone who you tell about it, someone who texts you every Tuesday when you get home—who you know would call, if you wanted her to. Some nights now, you don't drive home straightaway, you linger by your car to talk to one of the others. Sometimes you laugh together. Sometimes when you come home, you feel so light you dance, twirling and spinning in your living room and sometimes, as you're doing that—right as you're doing that—the rage comes and it never ceases to shock you, the power of the emotions colliding. You talk about it the next Tuesday, how you didn't know that could happen; feeling two different things at the exact same time.

When you stop going, it's not because you are finished, but because you're finished for now, you're finished enough. You are moving away—to New York, to the texting woman, to the next part of your life. Your tears are for saying goodbye and for leaving so much of yourself, such a big part of yourself, in the room. Your tears are for hope, for love. And for healing. And because after all this time, and all these Tuesdays, you can finally name what happened and know—really know—that the shame isn't yours to carry anymore.

And that it never was.

DUPLEX

JERICHO BROWN

A poem is a gesture toward home.
It makes dark demands I call my own.

    Memory makes demands darker than my own:
    My last love drove a burgundy car.

My first love drove a burgundy car.
He was fast and awful, tall as my father.

    Steadfast and awful, my tall father
    Hit hard as a hailstorm. He'd leave marks.

Light rain hits easy but leaves its own mark
Like the sound of a mother weeping again.

    Like the sound of my mother weeping again,
    No sound beating ends where it began.

None of the beaten end up how we began.
A poem is a gesture toward home.

SAWDUST

DAVID MOSCOVICH

This is the color of silence when Azuka calls you and says a pervert ejaculated on the back of her sweater on the crowded morning train and you throw on your jean jacket and you run past the endless construction cones up the stairs to Higashi Machi station and you push your way past the aging greysuit in line to speak to the attendants and you're getting the steel face from the station master, this is the color of silence when you tell him you know the perpetrator was wearing a bright orange shirt, you know there are video cameras, you know her train stopped at this station at 7:44AM, you know which train he took, even which track the train was on, you're pointing to the cameras all around, you know they understand when you say *chikan*, which could be translated, for all practical and impractical purposes, as Pervert Who Masturbates on Train, this is the color of silence when the attendant looks at you and does nothing, promises nothing, sympathizes with nothing you say and probably doesn't even believe you, the predacious outsider, when the attendant looks at you and sees only the problem of an angry foreign presence, a tumorous Dorothy, a raised lunatic exhorting in aggressive Japanese over a flaw in the system, there is nothing in place to defeat the epidemic of *chikan*, a word in Japanese that means groper, but everyone knows when you say the word you mean very precisely, Pervert Who Masturbates on Train, an epidemic which plagues the Nipponese archipelagos, a problem which will never be solved since people don't talk, cycles of shame, etc., saving face is more important, this is the silence of a very deep and true melancholia, the symptom of a sickness so ingrained into the culture that anyone bringing attention to the problem is viewed as bigger than the problem itself, the only problem here is not that of sexual harassment or unwanted touch, the only problem is that of losing face, which has been exacerbated by you, pointing out the problem of *chikan*, which is not a problem at all, as long as we ignore it and save our faces, the problem is you, foreign Quasimodo, this is also the color of silence Azuka received when the women on the train watched her with clinical discomfort and only shifted their bras, silently, and only blinked with mute, engorged eyes, as they witnessed the *chikan* spooging on her back, and decided that they shouldn't say anything since Azuka didn't know yet, they might embarrass her, or worse, themselves, or worse, the other important strangers on the train who might notice they opened their pretty mouths, wouldn't it stand to logic if one person can lose face, someone else could find it?

DOCTOR'S OFFICE FIRST WEEK IN THIS COUNTRY

JAVIER ZAMORA

it's procedure to inspect
the ass of an immigrant kid

undress put this gown on
the doctor will be here soon

that first day after Sonoran Desert
I showered for hours when we got to parents' apartment

Father showed me the way to turn the knob that first day
how things worked

I hadn't seen him since I was one
I didn't *know him* know him

this is how you make your pee-pee grow he said so it's bigger so
    it's the biggest
he said sometime that first month or that first year
pull
pull I did
pull
do it now
you're young it will work he said

did anything happen the doctor asked in front of my parents
then alone
did anything happen along the way in Spanish
all of this in Spanish
starting with *es procedimiento*

this is how you get hot water
twist then pull

no
I'd never used a sponge
soap-bar and hand was enough back there next to a well

I'd never seen a "shower"
parents said it that way in English *chá-uer*

that first "shower"
my dirt drew a dark rim around the linoleum

you will hear from us next week
I came back for all the necessary shots

I grew up across the street from a clinic
every kid cried

I came back I got shot I didn't cry

I kept turning the wrong knob
even after Dad showed me

then Mom showed me
then we showered together

to make me comfortable with my own body again
with theirs
with anyone's

it burned that first time
my skin
hot water
nothing happened

it burned
I'm sure
seguro que
nada pasó

DISPATCH FROM MY EARLY 20S

CATHERINE ESPOSITO PRESCOTT

Walking home alone, I held an antenna over every blind spot

haunted by stories of girls stolen, ghost-girls grabbed from streets

cloaked in shadow. I'd cross into lamplight, hold my breath around

corners, angle my head down, eyes cast just high enough to see out

but not make eye contact. I wanted no contact. I traveled with a look

that said *do not approach*, with a certain swagger, and I was safe.

In corporate offices and classrooms fluorescent lights made theft

transparent. If something of mine was stolen in bright light, it was *ok*

if only because it was seen. I dealt in intangibles, lost them daily:

an idea here, dignity there. How many leering eyes could my body
hold?

I had to want the win, the project, the promotion, the A without
letting it

show. Not in my smile, not in my smirk, not in my thigh-high
hemline.

Every girl owns an arsenal of eye rolls. As we grow, we learn how
to turn,

words into roses, then swords, when to strike, when to pivot and exit.

THE MAN WITH THE VIOLIN CASE

RUTH BEHAR

I was nineteen years old, working at a gallery in Manhattan that sold "primitive art." My job was to transcribe the business letters the owner spoke into a tape recorder. He was a decrepit and arrogant man and he confessed to me that most of the art he was selling at inflated prices had been robbed from archaeological sites in Mexico and Peru. I wanted to report him but didn't know how or to whom. In any case, the summer was about to end. I'd be returning to college and would never set foot in that gallery again.

I finished the last transcription of the day and slid into the crowded subway to return to my parents' apartment in Forest Hills, in the New York City borough of Queens. This was the working-class part of Forest Hills, near 108th Street, all nondescript apartments, filled with immigrants, far from the famed West Side Tennis Club and its historic championships. I had gone to junior high and high school in Forest Hills, and my parents still lived in the same apartment with the picture window that had needed to be smashed so their green velvet sectional sofa could be hoisted inside. The vertigo I'd felt seeing that gaping hole in the living room still made me dizzy thinking about it.

My younger brother was spending the summer in Boston, where he was studying music. My parents were also away for the weekend. I had the apartment to myself, which was unusual, and I was looking forward to the privacy and solitude. My traditional and gregarious Cuban father didn't like to see me spending hours immersed in a book in total silence. He wanted me to go to parties, to enjoy life. He thought education was wasted on girls. I had gone to college against his will. After a long day of selling textiles for a boss he detested, he would slip into bed to watch reruns of the *I Love Lucy* show, with the volume on so loud my ears hurt from the canned laughter accompanying Desi Arnaz's accented English. Silence frightened my father. Silence welcomed the demons. He said to me, "You're turning my house into a funeral parlor."

I was obsessed by philosophy in those days and had brought home a stack of books by Kierkegaard, Nietzsche, Sartre, and Simone de Beauvoir that I planned to finish before going back to school. I was looking forward to being on my own for a few days in the apartment to read for hours without feeling like a criminal.

Every seat on the subway was occupied during rush hour. I leaned against one of the poles, trying to stay clear of the men who tried to brush up against me. It was 1975, and the subway was an easy place for guys to enjoy a cheap erotic fantasy. I tried to read *Being and Nothingness* standing up, but it was awkward. The book was heavy and thick, and I kept losing my page.

I looked up and noticed a man staring at me. He wore a dusty suit and a white shirt open at the neck and scuffed shoes. He was carrying a violin case. I guessed he was about ten years older than me but didn't want to look too closely.

I turned away and tried to avoid his gaze, glancing at the signs posted in the subway and studying my red painted toenails.

I could feel his eyes on me. Without looking up, I could feel him devouring me with his eyes.

"You're overreacting," I told myself.

He was a violinist, no more harmful than my brother, who played the bass. Maybe he was going to teach or perform somewhere.

But why was he staring at me? I wasn't wearing anything flashy—a wrap-around summer dress, that tied at the waist, and platform sandals. My hair was pulled back into a tight bun. My only piece of jewelry was a simple gold ring with a heart in the center. It was made from my great-grandmother's gold tooth when I was a child in Havana and it still fit.

I figured he wouldn't attack me in the subway. There were too many people. As long as he didn't get off at my stop, everything would be fine, I reasoned.

He kept staring. I wished I could hide under a blanket. I suddenly understood how a woman might choose to conceal her face with a veil. I felt exposed, as if his gaze stripped me of my decency. I remembered finding my father's stash of *Playboys* when I was a girl and how it shocked me to see naked women posing so luridly and happily, inviting the gaze. But I didn't know where to look. The staring man held the violin case against his hip at a strange angle and it looked obscene.

The more he stared, the more nervous I grew. I became dizzy and began hyperventilating. What would happen if I passed out? Would I be taken to a dark alley and cut into pieces? I'd read about dismembered women who'd been butchered and left to rot in garbage cans. I waited anxiously for the train to arrive at my stop. All I wanted was to be able to breathe normally again.

People slowly left the train at one stop, then another, then another. As the crowd fell away, I felt even more vulnerable.

From the corner of my eye, I saw that he stayed where he was, staring at me intently, his other features remaining still.

If he took the slightest step toward me, I'd scream.

The train came to a screeching halt. At last it was my stop. Jumping off the train, I smelled the stink of piss and dead rats, the nauseating aroma of the subway in summer.

I rushed to the staircase and didn't look back for fear I'd turn to salt.

I could feel him close behind me on the stairs. Would he pinch my ass?

What was he really carrying in his violin case? A gun? A rope to strangle me? A whip to beat me? Knives to dismember me?

The violin case was grazing my feet and I quickened my pace not to trip on it.

I reached the top of the stairs and turned onto the street that I always took to go home. He was following me. He walked briskly, a few steps away.

It had gotten dark. The thick green leaves of the trees made a swishing sound in the summer breeze, like the whispers of bitter old women. I glanced nostalgically at Jahn's Ice Cream Parlor where my high school Spanish teacher, Mrs. Rodriguez, had treated me to a kitchen sink sundae as a reward for my studiousness. I had always been a good schoolgirl. Now that all seemed so long ago. I had a sinking feeling that my innocence would be snatched from me on this night, as the shadow of the man with the violin loomed ever closer at my heels.

What could I say to make him go away? If I spoke, he might respond, and I didn't want to hear his voice. I didn't want to look into his eyes. Was he a murderer? A rapist? Why was he following me?

I crossed the street and he crossed right behind me. I'd left the stores behind on Queens Boulevard and there was nowhere to stop and disappear into a crowd. As I got closer to my building it occurred to me, I shouldn't go inside. Then he'd know where I lived. He could come after me.

How comforting it would have been to know that Mami was in the kitchen frying *croquetas* in oil or Papa was in bed watching *I Love Lucy* reruns at full volume. But no, the apartment was empty, something I'd foolishly been looking forward to. The man with the violin case would follow me down the long dark hallway leading to our apartment and grab me as I turned the key in the door. He'd put his hand over my mouth, push me inside the apartment, and Mami and Papi would return home and find their dead daughter, their daughter who invited the angel of death by reading books every night in solitude instead of going out to parties and having fun as a young girl should.

I took a turn past my building and kept on walking.

He was right behind me. The violin case was so close I thought he'd strike me with it at any moment. What impressed me was how he moved without making a sound, yet I felt him there.

I walked several blocks past our building, crossed the street, with him still following me.

Then I took a deep breath and stopped at the revolving glass doors of a hospital near Queens Boulevard and pushed my way inside.

In the lobby, there was a stench of illness and the bleach that was being used to cover up the rank odor of bodies decomposing in hidden corridors.

I ran to the reception desk. "I'm being followed, and I'm scared," I said.

The woman, whose eyes looked yellow under the fluorescent lights, gazed at me strangely.

"A man with a violin case. I think he's still there."

I pointed toward the door.

The man was gone.

"What would you like me to do?" the woman asked.

"Can somebody walk me home?"

"We can't do that, dear. We're a hospital. Do you want to go to the emergency room?"

It was tempting. I knew I'd be safe in the emergency room.

"Why don't you take a taxi? I can call one for you."

I agreed. I had a few dollars in my purse.

As the taxi drove me around the block to my building, I kept expecting to see the man with the violin case. I looked for him in the lobby. In the elevator. In the hallway. Inside the apartment. In the closets. Under the bed. Behind the curtains.

Over the next two days I was so spooked I couldn't sleep, couldn't shower, couldn't eat, couldn't read a single book. I was on high alert, watching day turn into night and night into day. I didn't leave the apartment, waiting anxiously for my parents to return. I kept looking through the peephole of our front door, convinced I'd see the man with the violin case standing there looking at me. He disappeared like a ghost, but the palpable fear he awoke in me still haunts me to this day.

GRABBED VILLANELLE

CATHERINE ESPOSITO PRESCOTT

Those lessons begin early, no doubt.
He takes. She gives. He grabs. She kicks.
A girl learns how to tune him out

when he says he can't live without
the smell of her hair, her hands on his stick.
Those lessons begin early, no doubt

on the high school bus, too loud to shout,
on the field, at home, it happens quick.
A girl learns how to tune him out

when he calls her *bitch* for walking out,
cunt, *prude*, *cold* as his prick.
Those lessons begin early, no doubt

survival is a sprint around the playground,
No, you can't kiss me. I feel sick.
A girl learns how to tune him out,

when the first boy leers at her and shouts,
her eyes well, her stomach turns to brick.
Those lessons begin early, no doubt.
A girl's gotta learn how to tune him out.

TENEMENT TRICK

VANESSA GARCIA

We were in college, we should have known better. We were drunk.
Me, Jessica and Yanik. I can't even remember the joint where we
met him, somewhere on the Lower East Side. As for the guy,
he was just a guy, a short-haired, young urban professional with
an apartment he could loan us to brush off our beers. No sex,
just a layover to tonic our gins. That was the promise. There was
only one bathroom in the hallway, he said. The place, it used to
be a tenement. We were curious. We'd been learning, in class,
about early migration waves to The City; the first Jews, and the
sweatshops of 1900. The whole floor still shared a toilet, he said,
if we were ok with that we could surf the wave of his couch for
the night, until the morning. He seemed nice. We were used to
shared bathrooms, we lived in dorms, so we said: alright.

On the way to his place, Yanik threw up in the cab. She
passed out on the promised-land couch. Jessica and I were led to
the bed instead. Just to sleep, we slurred. Sleep, that's all, we said.
That was our contract, our handshake, our pact. Still he groped
us, while we said No, please leave us alone. Under the covers,
we fought off fingers, hands, and whispers. Not sure where we
were, and with Yanik passed out on the couch, immovable, we
were waiting for the light, to pick up our shit and take flight.
Which we did, leaving him, finally, asleep. On the subway, we felt
the dank ding and the echo of him, the one-window tenement
settling its weight on us. We looked at each other, tired. It was
summer, and the rays were bright but already beating.

YELLOW AMERICAN WOMAN

MARCI CALABRETTA CANCIO-BELLO

I see
you looking
at me
thinking
I don't
see you
looking at
my narrow
hips my too
straight hair
my almond
my monolid
my black
black eyes
and you
thinking I
must be in
such good
shape and
me thinking
you mean that
for the girl
whose blond
light always
catches eyes
and words
but then
realizing
you mean it

for me
because now
you're saying
I speak
English
so well
thinking I
don't get what
you're really
saying
thinking
I won't say
can't say
anything
against you
in your
language
that my body
can't say better
but now
I see you
thinking
you don't
understand
why I'm
yelling
so loud so
resistant
so you turn
pink and
your eyes
narrow
at me not
looking

at me
not looking
at my
small
American
mouth not
asking
why you're
so scared
of me
now.

POPPONESSET

EILEEN MYLES

I guess I was about 18 and I was in a car driving down the Southeast Expressway towards Cape Cod. We had just had our Biology exam and I was immensely relieved. The sky was a pale blue like it is in late afternoon. I had a tall can of beer in my hand and it seems I see me in profile. How strange. I was riding in Louise's car, a black Mustang. She was a short athletic constantly tanned girl. I had a strange feeling of excitement around Louise which compelled me to fulfill her idea of me. It didn't seem too bad. She saw me as intelligent, I think, and she laughed at me in a way that implied I was a riot. I didn't know for a fact that she thought I was good looking, but here I was in a carload of girls heading down the Cape to a party at Louise's family's house in Popponesset. We were going for the express purpose of meeting other friends of hers, guys. Ones she had gone to high school with and she described them as hunks, or something like that, and it was perfect in her mind that they meet me and Anne who we also knew from school. And being from Lexington they already knew Sally and Diane and we were going to have fun. I felt extremely passive about it, exhausted from the exam and sort of apprehensive at the idea of meeting them. It seemed destined that they wouldn't like me, there seemed to be something missing. I often thought different guys to be quite beautiful and I would watch the way they walked and moved their hands and leaned and held things and looked around.

We got down to Louise's house and we brought our huge amounts of beer in from the car and our small amounts of clothes. We had big bags of Doritos and stuff. Bunches of cigarettes. We threw ourselves down in the soft family beach furniture and proceeded to talk, just us girls in the fading light. I wasn't intending to smoke, was off them for several months now and had been through the hard part, which was gaining weight, and now that I had done a little of that, everything tasted good and I could breathe pretty well and so it was a big mistake to begin now.

I watched the smoke curl up in the air through the windows of the beach house and I grew immensely intelligent and witty as I tended to in a group of girls, not being afraid after a couple of drinks that anyone would be embarrassed by my intensity. They were intense too. It was a big secret to everyone and we hid it well and let it out now and then when we were drunk, that we were smart and cared and thought about many things. Diane had long dark hair and she also held court I noticed, and she held her cigarette like an older woman when she spoke, and I figured she was probably turning into her mother or someone else.

They're here, shrieked Louise. "Dave," she yelled strutting out and it was apparent Louise was quite drunk. Everyone was. I remember being quiet for a couple of minutes like someone told me to shut up, no let me be frank I barely remember a thing. I was walking on the beach with Kit, Kit Anderson was his name and he had on a red sweater and we had been talking maybe a little bit inside and I had no feeling he liked me at all, in fact he was holding me up and I felt burdensome and he felt like the boys from Arlington only I didn't know this guy at all and he was a big blond. I remember we were trying to make out, but that was boring and pointless because I was so drunk plus, we didn't care about each other at all. He was probably drunk too but I don't know. I went into the bedroom with Kit and then it began. I don't know. Just a rhythm of many guys, I seem to remember all of them in there at once but that may have been a blur and then precisely Dave sitting down, a therapist's son, Dave Margolis something like that and he was dark haired and he was sitting on the other bed saying you are disgusting, you are a slut. It was like being drugged in the dentist's office. I felt fat, I remember loathing my body. It went on and on, people on top of me, feeling scared, feeling turned on. Am I dreaming? Rape was the first sex I ever heard of. Some girl tied to a telephone pole down by Spy Pond. It seemed to always happen in nature. Choking. I had a lot of cocks shoved in my mouth. Hoots. Getting fucked with cold hot dogs. There was pancake batter all over the place. I remember my wool plaid pants being off. Being white. It was cold.

Dave was talking to me like it was my fault. I was trying to talk, but my tongue was so thick. That underwater feel. You're an asshole. Um not. The door was slightly open into the kitchen and light was flooding in through a crack. Louise's brother was on top of me and I could see a little smile on his face, and he was sucking my tit. He's happy. How weird. He was hurting me, and it felt pretty good. He had his glasses off. I pretended I was asleep.

In the morning everyone girls were sleeping in clumps all over the house. I had my own bedroom it seemed. I was alone. So sick. Tried to make some coffee. Gave up and walked down to the beach. There were these polyps, pink and translucently fleshy, scattered all over the little tan beach. I sat on the side of an old rowboat. I felt like the inside of my head had been scooped out. I was painfully numb. I had been raped, right? Even if I don't know exactly what happened. That's how I feel. A bunch of good-looking suburban guys, 18 or 19, same as me, who all owned cars, trashed me for two reasons: I was drunk, they didn't know me. I wrote my name on the sand with my toe. EILEEN MYLES. Yes, that's who I am. I rubbed it out with my foot.

How are you feeling, Leena? I was standing in the kitchen trying to make some coffee. Louise explained that she thought I liked it, that's why she didn't interfere. Sally had passed out. "Those guys are assholes, Leena." Anne just said she was scared. She didn't know them either. Diane went out for pizza with, I can't remember his name. I wasn't ever going to drink again, but I felt safe at the card party that night. The beers helped me relax.

People were kind of taking care of me then. But Eddy, Louise's brother, just killed me. So righteous about what a bunch of little pricks they were. I went out with him a few times after that—we saw Vanilla Fudge. I wanted to see if his story would ever crack. Louise must've known he fucked me too. Once she pulled into a gas station in Lexington where Dave worked. She didn't warn me. Louise. Hi Dave. Hey Louise. He can't see you. I'm sure he doesn't even remember. Hey Dave! She got out of the car.

THAT AUTUMN SUNDAY

GERRY LAFEMINA

The weeds genuflected all around the clearing
as if a sacrifice had to be given, &

the man with the knife
the man who zipped up, laughed

in a way some might be tempted
to over dramatize, &

turned away, so the wind that remained
seemed to *tsk* its tongue as if to shame

until even the sun lowered its brilliant head.

DAUGHTER, THEY'LL USE
EVEN YOUR OWN GAZE
TO WOUND YOU

BETH ANN FENNELLY

1. CHICAGO, IL

My high school teacher loved that I loved libraries, so she promised she'd bring me to her alma mater's. One Saturday, we took the train in and she donned white gloves to turn manuscript pages while I roamed the stacks, inhaling that dear dusty library funk. Wait: did I hear footsteps? When I was sure I'd been mistaken, I pulled out a heavy tome. There, thrusting through, a tube of flesh. Years later a librarian would tell me paraphilic activity is quite common in her place of work. Just in case you're wondering if I was special.

2. SOUTH BEND, IN

My college roomies and I were three beers in, walking from campus to Brigit's, a bar so seedy that, after graduation, it'd be condemned. A Tercel pulled over and the interior light flicked on to halo a man consulting a map. Good Catholics, we inquired if he needed directions. *Can you show me where I am on my map?* So, we stepped closer and discovered where he was on his map: through the center, dickly. I'm guessing it was Denise who began laughing, or maybe Beth, but in seconds we were all hooting, we could barely stumble away, shrieking and pounding one another. He screeched through the intersection, the light still red.

3. FAYETTEVILLE, AR

From dawn till noon I'd reviewed Wordsworth, cramming for
my comp exam, and now as I ran through the park, sonnets
metered out my pounding feet. A bicycle came from behind, a
man swiveling to see my face. At the top of the hill, he stopped,
turned, and coasted back toward me. I could see his fist gripping
something low on his belly. What zinged through my head:
a bouquet. But that was no bouquet. I didn't even slow as he
passed, just averted my eyes.

I'd run nine miles that day with one to go.
I guess I'd learned by then what women know.

BINGO NIGHT FOR MISSING AND EXPLOITED CHILDREN

M. B. MCLATCHY

Before we went underground. Before you fell through a gyre with no
 sound.

If one piece were unwound. If you had run. If we had looked for
 you sooner. If you had screamed. If the gods had intervened.

Nascent. Still blooming, the orchid on your window sill. A thrill
 of color.

Gone. Gone. Gone. Gone. Gone. Phantom limb. If the soul
 leaves the body, we did not feel it go. Nothing and everything
 cloistered in stone.

Omens we left for others. Ripples on a resting pond.
The whistling of a breeze. The imprint on the ovaries.

105 DEGREES, SOUTH

LUCIA LEAO

The secret is to kill it right,
but that summer doesn't die.
Remember, it was there, where men
still pump gas into our cars,
deliver their jokes, make eye contact.

Your hair, oily, and mine,
the seats gluing our laughs,
our thighs, driving
to my first home, your house,
and although they could help us, you said,
"Let's get some air outside," forgetting
our dresses were transparent with sweat.

Remember the way
they could see us?
I do.

EPISTLE FROM THE HOSPITAL
FOR HARASSMENT

JENNY MOLBERG

to B.L.

As in a house of mourning / cover the mirrors / Save yourself
from yourself / Open the windows / Feed your history to the
night / Do not wrestle / against your story / let it keep happening
/ then kill it— / the poet who invited you for coffee / a manila
folder of poems / meticulously typed / and tucked beneath your
arm / all those beats and breaks / silenced / as he thrust his hand
on your hip, saying *Sweetheart, try your hair in a bun* / and *What
about glasses / If you wore glasses men wouldn't notice you so much* /
Or your colleague who poked / a bruise on your thigh / guessing
at its origins / Or the man who made the bruise / *Honey, you're
not as stupid as you look*— / Cast it out / until the night is so full
of the feathers of your thoughts / it grows the giant wings of a
crow / takes off— / Now lie before the curtained mirrors / Forget
what you look like / For better is a wandering eye / than the two
you clench shut / waiting for him to finish

IN SUPPORT OF VIOLENCE

CHRISTOPHER SOTO

> *Two hundred Indian women killed their rapist*
> *on the courtroom floor of Nagpur in 2004.*
> *When police tried to arrest lead perpetrators // the women*
> *responded "arrest us all."*

=

In this windowless room // where he poured acid & stole money
// arrest us all
In this windowless room [shut like the gut of an ox] arrest us all

Gored & gorge are words to describe a wound   Gorgeous // the
opening
Of a blade inside his chest   *Gorgeous* // black galaxies, growing

Across his skin, we threw rocks & chili
pepper
Arrest us all

On the railroad tracks // where he murdered our sisters & left their
dead bodies
On the railroad tracks // where black ants began // biting crowns into

Calves //   The world is spinning and we're // falling
from its bed
How could we mourn?   He kept killing // & threatening // &
raping us

Arrest us all
                              On the red puddle // on the white
                                                 courthouse floor
Arrest us all
                              We sawed his penis off // & tore his house
                                                 // to rubble

Look // the streets are swarming // in protests   [welcome home]
             The night is neon & buzzing like bumble-bees

We never wanted to kill // only to stay alive // &
We waited like virgins // for the gentleness of strangers // to help or
                                                 empathize.

CREATION STORY

MIA LEONIN

At age nineteen the Black community translated my white body
    for me:
You. Can't. Be. White. You

who got some extra lovin' on you. You,
ham hock booty.

On Troost Avenue, men rubbernecked and crashed,
a five-car pile-up from looking at my ass.

And me—head down, eyes glued to cracked sidewalk
face hot with shame. And me—
wearing a red, A-line skirt that hit mid-calf.

Years later, my husband explains, *You can't cover that up.*
A year after, a lover explains, *Men know what's there,*
even if they can't see it. That's their second sight, their sixth sense.

Black folks translated my white body for me.
Then Cubans did. *Criollita original!*
Negra vestido de blanco!
Gracias a la virgin por este culo.
From construction hangars, convertibles, and solares,
they hissed and whined and moaned.

I took a good, long look at my face:

my honey-splattered face, my cowrie-shell face, my calculus-
meets-physics face, my Neptune-trined-with-Saturn face,

my split-second, gut-instinct, don't-go-with-him face, my
Venus-in-Cancer face, my wanna-burn-every-war-monger-
at-the-stake face, my wanna-nurse-every-baby-ever-
racked-with-hunger face, my Yeah, I'm-buying-condoms.
What-the-fuck-are-you-staring-at? face, my Uh huh, I-wanna-
have-sex-and-I'm-not-interested-in-reproduction-so-dispense-
with-the-dirty-looks-and-write-the-prescription face, my
wanna-put-every-war-monger-on-trial face, my wanna-strip-
down-naked-and-stand-in-front-of-a-military-tank face, my
ven-pa'ca-porque-te-quiero-comer face, my abandonment-
issues-for-days face, my inner-child-before-it-was-a-pop-
psychology-term face, my cowardly face, my fear-of-retribution
face, my please-don't-take-this-little-piece-of-mountain-I've-
managed-to-molehill-into-a-beautiful-windowsill-garden face,
my I'm-through-with-molehilling face, my turns-out-I-am-
the-mountain face.

I took a long, long look at my face
and I decided that it was good.

So I tossed that that mug, that kisser, that visage,
I tossed her to the horizon for safe keeping.

I fixed my gaze on her and I started walking.
This was the beginning of resting bitch face.

ANGEL HEART
IN ISTANBUL

CAITLIN GRACE MCDONNELL

We wanted an American movie
to take our minds off the sensory
excess of the spice markets, men
calling out to us, *Elma Cayi, Excuse ma'am
you dropped your hat.* Mickey Rourke
had been in *Diner.* Lisa Bonet on *Cosby.*
Cigarette smoke wafted through the dark
as her naked body gleamed and writhed
with blood and snakes. When the lights
came on, all men. *You shouldn't be
walking here at night*, a guy our age
said to us as we hurried home.
There was someone behind us
like a thick dusty curtain closing.
As I sped up, a hand reached
between my legs and squeezed.
Fist like a muscled flower, a
hungry clamp. My body froze
as my sister's turned around.
All that power she'd stored up
as our father used her body
like a chess piece on the soccer field;
all the times she'd pinned me down
like we see our fathers do.
Get. The. Fuck. Away. From. Her,
she yelled from the bottom of it all,
and he took off like he'd seen

his own demons spring to life.
My body slowly returning to itself,
retching and surfacing in our rented
room, my sister's and my young
skin glowing with recognition:
what we could have
in this wretched world
and what we couldn't.

LAYOVER

JERICHO BROWN

Dallas is so
Far away
Even for the people
Who live
In Dallas a hub
Through which we get
To smaller places
That lurch
And hurt going
Home means stopping
In Dallas and all are
From little
Towns and farms
If all keep
Heading back
Far enough pay
Attention keep
Your belongings
Near everyone
In Dallas is
Still driving
At 3:24 a.m.
Off I-20 where
I was raped
Though no one
Would call it
That he was
Hovering by
The time

I understood
He thought it necessary
To leave me with knowledge
I can be
Hated I was
Smaller then
One road went
Through me
No airport
I drove
Him home
A wreck
On the freeway
We sat
In traffic
My wallet
On the seat
In between
My legs

WHEN IN MADAGASCAR

VICKI HENDRICKS

On a trip to celebrate my sixtieth birthday, a friend and I had a stopover in Antananarivo, the capitol, for three days. We paid a driver to show us craft markets and lemurs in a preserve. We passed laundry staked out to dry on every plot of grass, and islands of clay bricks, burning to harden, in every small lake, the means to build homes. We waited, amazed, while a six-year-old boy drove his 400-pound, long-horned zebu steer across the road.

In town, we became accustomed to traffic crawling amid hundreds of beggars who risked their feet to reach into our car for a trickle of change. On foot, as forewarned, we were surrounded by boys, aged nine or ten, chanting, their caps held open at our chests to distract from their fingers ravaging our lower pockets and unzipping our backpacks. We smacked their little hands away, startled by our swift, harsh response. They got nothing.

My only time alone, I walked down a side street, to a T-shirt shop, while my friend sipped her drink on the hotel balcony. A school let out, teens in their miraculously white, pressed shirts and blue pants and skirts, surely having come that morning from crowded, dirt-floored huts without water. They roiled over the sidewalk and flowed around me, a sweaty, old-lady tourist in her long-sleeved, 50 SPF shirt, pants, and pastel hat—a lump in their path. Except to one, a laughing boy with dark playful eyes. He reached out and grabbed for my crotch, just missing the mark, accepting empty air. I smacked his hand away, choked out some kind of laugh . . . an embarrassed laugh . . . a laugh of amazement . . . at my age . . .

In a country where half the population is under fifteen, and the average family of nine lives in a one-room hut; where a shirtless boy with a burn-scarred chest is his mother's best hope to retrieve a few coins; where boney, blistery-faced five-year-olds are strapped with infants on their backs each morning to beg— why do I remember that grab?

Forests of lemurs, the international attraction, are mostly ravaged. Wood is the only fuel for cooking and heat; selling it roadside, a meager sustenance for many. In the hills, with a single water pipe per village, women sit on hard red clay, lined up all day to fill plastic buckets from a trickle. The inland lake is polluted and fished-out; the ocean also depleted. Yet a beach community, struggling to market essential oils, cooked for me, as their lunch guest, a whole fish. My stomach grinds with the memory.

So, yes, there was that youthful hand thrust at me on a lark— such small change. I'd held out hope with my "rich" presence. No, you can't save them all. I didn't save any.

THE OPPOSITE OF MONSTERS

LAURA LEE HUTTENBACH

In September 2006, I was in the second month of a five-month backpacking trip up the east coast of Africa. I was 24 years old, traveling with a college friend named Markus, who was tall and blue-eyed. We'd just arrived in Dar es Salaam, the capital of Tanzania, and were staying at Mikadi Beach Lodge, a beachside campsite. After setting up our tent on the first day, at dusk, Markus and I decided to go for a run along the beach.

We turned right when we got to the Indian Ocean. Carrying nothing, we ran in the sand. We passed a sign. The sign was gray and wooden, with WARNING written in white letters, and two yellow triangles flanking both sides. Each yellow triangle contained a black exclamation point. Below, the sign read: YOU ARE ABOUT TO LEAVE MIKADI CAMP SECURITY ZONE. BE AWARE. But we didn't see that sign.

We ran maybe a mile down the beach and passed few people before turning around. When we were a quarter mile from the campsite, three young Tanzanian men approached us. They were probably teenagers—eighteen or nineteen. I don't remember what they were wearing or the details of their appearance, but I do remember one saying, in English, "Hello friends." But before I could smile and begin a conversation, one of them grabbed me. He grabbed me on the right side of my collarbone and slipped his fingers under the strap of my tank top and sports bra. The other two went after Markus. "Give us your camera," they shouted. We didn't have a camera. "Give us your money," they said. We had no money. "We will kill you," they said.

Markus tried to punch one of them, and that made the guy attached to my neck angry. This is when we both saw that he had a machete. The machete had a straight, black blade. He lunged at me, and I dove the other way. One of my hands dropped in the sand, and I pushed back up. The guy started swinging me around like a violent game of ring-around-the-rosie, and he was trying to get me to fall down. I think I was screaming. I don't remember who first suggested it, but suddenly Markus and I were yelling, "Take our shoes. Take our running shoes." The young men looked at our shoes—mine were new cross trainers that had cost ninety dollars at REI—and said, "Okay, give us your shoes."

We both ripped off our shoes and threw them in the sand. We sprinted back to the campsite. Shaky and bruised with fingerprints around my collarbone, I went to the lodge's reception. We told the employees what had happened, and to call the police. They laughed at us. The police, they said, would perhaps write up a police report, but that would cost us. And there was no way that the police would catch the criminals. They said, in exact words I can't remember, that *we* were the stupid ones to run—to leave the protection of the campsite—at dusk. *Why would you run on a deserted beach at night?* We were lucky, they said, to have only lost our shoes.

That night, my mind flipped through alternative endings to the story. I asked myself, "What if I had gone running alone?" I felt scared and insecure—meaning unsafe, but the word was slippery, like it could easily morph into meaning less confident, too. I don't like to admit it, but I wanted to be in the arms of a strong man who would protect me from bad guys.

The next day, riding aboard Kigamboni Ferry to Dar es Salaam, I noticed I had changed. I was jumpy. I hated being in a big crowd. I started seeing groups of Tanzanian teenagers as potential threats. In Tanzania, of course, Tanzanian teenagers are everywhere. I wanted to stop my mind from taking those images and turning them into suspicions.

The loss of my shoes presented a practical problem, too: I was on my way to climb Kilimanjaro, Africa's tallest mountain, covered by glacial ice fields, and I now had only sandals. I started asking around where I might be able to buy good sneakers. One person suggested that I just buy my old sneakers back. Just go to the nearby market, he said. The thieves probably sold your trainers to someone there.

I bought a cell phone so I could keep in touch with my family back home. Before the machete, I'd wanted to get off the grid. After, I wanted to be able to call for help. The first time I spoke with my brother, tears streamed down my face. But I didn't tell him what happened. I didn't want my family to worry, to think that all of Africa was Mikadi Beach after sunset.

A few days later, I was in Moshi Town, a base town where many climbers begin their ascent up Kilimanjaro, and I met a man named Zamo who worked for the Porters' Assistance Project, an NGO whose mission is to improve working conditions for the porters. When I told Zamo what had happened to my shoes, he offered me a pair of running shoes that a Danish couple had given to him. The shoes didn't fit him, and he felt bad about my experience. He said he hoped my impression of his country would improve. He also let me borrow other equipment—hiking poles, boots, and a jacket that kept me warm.

For the next three months, through Uganda, Kenya, Ethiopia, and Egypt, I walked in the shoes Zamo had given me. I met many people who were kind and gentle. But I had trouble going running by myself. When I heard footsteps behind me, my breath caught in my throat. Whenever my eyes caught a glimpse of a machete's black, straight blade, I panicked. Machetes are a common agricultural tool throughout Africa, and you see them everywhere in rural areas.

I recognized that those three Tanzanian teenagers attacked us for our money. Many Western travelers pour into African cities before they leave on safaris, and they carry cameras around their neck worth more than the country's per capita GDP. It's understandable, though not excusable, that, at some point, some teenagers with no expensive camera will ask, "How can I get a piece of what they have?"

It's tricky, I guess. Because when you are grabbed, you need to make sure that the experience doesn't keep grabbing you and hold you hostage for the rest of your life. You need to let the person who grabbed you go.

I won't run again at Mikadi Beach, but I run by myself all the time. I try to avoid dusk or night, because that is when the memories remind me they are still intact. In New York City, walking home at night, I am nervous. There is a difference between being safe and feeling safe, and I don't always feel safe. I'm not sure if that's because I got mugged or that's because I am a woman, walking alone in the street, and that makes me a target.

The guy that grabbed me was some form of a monster, and the lesson of my experience is not that some people can be monsters. That seems obvious. My personal task is to keep that monster as an individual, and not to see characteristics of his person in another person who has nothing to do with him. Every one of us has had monsters in our life, but societies break down when we fear people who look like our monsters, but who, in fact, are the opposite of monsters.

THE WORLDS WORDS MAKE

ZOE WELCH

THE 60S

1

I'm six. I'm in someone's basement suite. My mom is there, and other people. I'm in the bathroom. I'm facing the tiled wall above the bathtub. My right arm is stretched out behind me, to where my hand has been grabbed. P places my hand on his penis. P is friends with the people in the living room.

I'm riding the bus with my father, which is an activity we often do together during our visits. We're sitting on the long bench at the back of the bus. My father asks if P has ever done anything to me. I say no.

2

I'm eight. I'm walking to school. Halfway there, two blocks from home, in the lane behind the church, a man turns toward me. He locks eyes with me and opens his coat. He's naked. He's moving his hands up and down his body. I run.

3

See The 00s, 10.

4

I'm fifteen. I have a summer job sailing a "small ship" in a man-made pond at the summer fair, reenacting the Anglo-Spanish War with other teenagers. F is in charge. F is married with a small daughter.

After work each day, F stays behind with us small ship sailors. He drives us to the beach, or to a park. He buys us alcohol that we drink with him in his car. At the end of these "parties," F drives us home, first dropping off the boys, one by one, then me. I'm always last. In front of my building F tells me that he and his wife have agreed that they can have sex with other people. I don't move. I say nothing.

5

I'm seventeen. It's afternoon. It's sunny. It's late spring. I'm downtown, on my way to work. I'm wearing a loose peasant top. As I walk down the sidewalk, a man thrusts his hand inside my shirt as he passes by. I think it's my fault.

I arrive at work and T is there. He's the regional manager. He's a draft dodger. He's married with two small children and his wife is pregnant with their third child. T says he can tell, through my shirt, that my areolas are light coloured. I'm not sure what an areola is but feel like it shouldn't be spoken about like this.

6

I'm twenty. I'm at college. I'm coming home from class one night. As I exit the bus, I glance around, as I always do, to see who's staying on and who's getting off. I don't know where I learned to do this. As the doors are closing behind me, I see a man jump up and exit the bus too. I take note.

The bus pulls away, and I cross the main thoroughfare and begin walking. The man heads in the same direction on the other side of the street, walking a few steps behind me. I'm approaching my turn, and I gradually slow my pace so the man will cross the side street before I do. He does, and I dart down the street, quickly looking over my shoulder. The man is running across the thoroughfare in my direction. I bolt. I look for a house with the lights on inside, a sign someone's home. The man turns the corner, running towards me. A few doors down, I open the gate to a house with lights on and I bang on the front door. As the door opens, the man runs past the house, penis in hand, masturbating. I tell the man at the door what's happening and why I'm there. My own house is three blocks away. He lets me use the phone to call my roommates, who leave immediately in a pack to come escort me home. As I wait, I tell the whole story to the man in whose house I've sought safety. He tells me he believes everyone has a right to live the way they want.

7

I'm twenty-three. I'm in a new city and staying with M until I can find my own place. M and I are friends but were once a couple. M lives in an unfinished loft above a restaurant. He pays no rent in return for his work to complete construction on the loft. There's a mattress on the floor in one corner. We share it. I wake one morning as I'm climaxing. M is between my legs. I choke on my own rage. I say nothing.

8

I'm twenty-five. I'm in a film course. I make a silent short called *No Sound Reason* about a woman walking down city streets, sensing the unseen threats all around her. In class we talk about our projects, about their genesis, about our intentions. I talk about walking alone at night with my keys inserted between my fingers to make a kind of jagged fist, dagger-like. I talk about walking with a match in one hand and the matchbook in the other, ready to strike the match against the flint strip, ready to flick fire in an assailant's face. I don't know how I know to do this. My film instructor, a gentle man, has never heard of such a thing. He's shocked.

THE 90S

9

I'm thirty-three. I have very short hair. Extensions are just hitting the scene. It's summer. A stylist I know offers to give me a full head of hair. We spend the whole day together at his salon. It's fun. I leave with long blond hair falling down my back. I've never had hair this long. I get on my bike to peddle home. I hear calling. I hear more calling. I realize they're calling at me. Hey baby. Hey baby. Hey baby.

THE 00S

10

I'm forty-two. The traumas are surfacing. I'm in counselling, which means going back. The memories are dark and distant. I feel them inside me in a place I've never felt before, a place I don't want to go to. That place is tight and hard. It's where I'm still in the basement, in the house where my mom and I were boarders when I was little. I'm alone. I'm tied up. I-J, the landlady, is upstairs in the kitchen. My mom is in our bedroom on the floor above that. She's unwell and can't look after me. She's medicated and asleep and can't hear anything. I'm in the basement where I-J keeps me. I-J says no one will believe me if I say anything, and we'll be on the street if I do. I tell no one.

THE 00S

11

I'm fifty-six. I work with inner city high school students on a zines program. One of the zines has the image of a girl on the cover; we see her in profile, from waist to knees, dressed in a skirt; in her hand we see keys jutting through her fingers. The zine is called *Rape Culture*. The girl who made it is in front of me. I find her eyes, and I tell her: Me too.

IN GUIDING DRAGON-WASP BEHAVIOR OF DEVIANT TENTACLES BENEATH THE UNDERSKIRT OF AN UNSUSPECTING QUEEN

CATHERINE MOORE

Note: drones will be drones
and drakes will be drakes—this
matters not if only we would
prevent girls from being.

THE SHAPE OF OTHER PEOPLE

KELLY SUNDBERG

The river unfolded, dark and seamless, in a ribbon below the A-frame in the Idaho wilderness where I worked for the US Forest Service. Inside the A-frame, on the surface of the couch, was the imprint of a body. "Who died?" I had joked to my coworker Emily when I first saw the imprint. "There's a chalk outline on the couch."

Emily shrugged. "That was just me," she said. "It was 115 degrees in my bedroom. I thought it would be cooler out here, so I slept on the couch, but I woke up covered in sweat."

I looked at that salty outline and wondered if I could fit my own body inside of it, if I could make my soft curves fit into Emily's lean shadow. I was, it seemed, always fitting myself into the shape of other people.

=====

After leaving my ex-husband, it took driving almost 4,000 miles across the country and living in that A-frame outside of my hometown to feel safe. I was 35 and had returned to a seasonal job in my hometown where I worked as a wilderness ranger. The Forest Service is an institution dominated by openly sexist men, but I could handle those men. It was my ex-husband's charm, his "I'm such a good guy" schtick that still terrified me.

=====

When it finally got too hot for me in the A-frame, I sprayed the black couch with cleaner and eased myself into the space another woman had made for me. Emily had become a good friend who helped me feel safe again, but even she couldn't teach me how to keep myself safe from the monsters inside of me.

Five years later, after I'd completed my PhD and published a memoir about my abusive marriage, I returned to my hometown for Christmas. I met Emily for a drink and told her about the man I had been seeing. I had broken up with him a few weeks earlier. I told Emily that he was kind, smart, and funny, but he had an inability to articulate emotions. Still, I said wistfully, "He always made me feel safe."

Emily took a drink, looked straight in my eyes, and said, "Is safety worth that much to you?"

———

Later that evening, I received a text from a different man, a man who had always been brilliant at articulating his feelings and making me feel special, but who also had an emotional affair with me while he was in a committed relationship with someone else. I'd ended things with him when he didn't break up with that person. I'd used the words, "You are a shitty person." I meant it, but I also knew that I was projecting my own shame on to him.

He and I weren't in contact anymore, but that night in my hometown when I met up with Emily, he sent me a text letting me know that, if I was in town, he was in town too. He said he just wanted to give me the heads-up in case we ran into each other. I had—after all—called him a shitty person.

I texted him back and said that I wasn't angry anymore.

———

Hours later, we were fucking, and it hurt. "It hurts," I said.

He stopped. "Wait, did you just say that it hurts?" he asked.

Something in me shrank. "No," I said.

"Oh, good," he said, and resumed what he was doing.

It hurt.

The morning after, I called the man who had made me feel safe. I told him that I missed his gentleness. I asked if we could try again. He said yes.

I had thought that healing would be a straight line, but healing is more like a squiggle. I am trapped somewhere in a curve.

A reader of my book gifted me with three sessions with an "emotional alchemist." It was the most "woo" thing I had ever done, but I was desperate.

I spoke on the phone with the alchemist, and she asked if she could tap into my energy, so that she could "shift" it. The process was somewhat like Reiki but more intense, and though I was a skeptic, I wanted to believe.

She had cards, and she asked them for answers. She perceived a tenseness in my throat, and she asked what it was. The cards told her that it was despair. She then asked me for permission to shift that despair, and maybe it was psychosomatic, but I felt a loosening in my throat. That was in the first session. In the next session, we talked about my mother, the novel I'm working on, and my creative energy. She shifted things, and I started writing again.

And in the third and final session, we talked about men. There was anger, so much anger. At one point, she said, "Are you taking notes?" I answered that I was. She then instructed me to start writing and rant about the men I was angry at. I wrote quietly that I was angry at my father for not making me feel valued. I wrote that I was angry at my ex-husband for making me feel valued then hurting me anyway. I wrote that I was angry at the man who had hurt me during sex because I felt he was "hate fucking" me.

As I was writing about that man—still quietly—the alchemist said, "Wait, there is a lot of anger here. It is not yours." I had not told her what I was writing about.

She said, "Someone else has given you their anger. I want you to say this after me, 'Any anger that was given to me, and that is not mine, I return to the source with loving kindness and compassion.'"

I felt a loosening again.

"Whoa," she said. "That was a lot of anger."

I knew that his wasn't the only man's anger I had internalized.

＝

I used to be a chalk outline that was filled with men's anger. My life could never be my own. I was always trying to fit into the shape of other people.

＝

At the end of our session, the alchemist asked the cards if there was any other energy she needed to clear. Suddenly, she grew quiet for a moment. "It's horror," she said.

She said, "There are things you don't even remember. You are holding on to so much."

I had flashes of what had been done to me by men—being pinned down, being spat upon, being hit, being grabbed, being hurt.

Being hurt, and hurt, and hurt some more.

Horror is not meant to be contained in one's own body.

"You've been holding on to that horror because you didn't want it to happen again, but you've learned what you needed to learn," she said.

"You need to let it go now."

———

In my memoir, rivers are a motif. I grew up next to the largest undammed river in the Lower 48. I worked on the same river for the forest service while I lived in that A-frame with the chalk outline. There is a moment in the book where my ex-husband is swept into the icy river while trying to rescue our dog, and I fear that I will lose them both forever. I didn't lose them that day, but I did eventually lose them both.

There are other moments in the book where I looked at the dark water rushing by and thought, I could jump.

I wanted to be swept into that current, for the dark water to drown out the horror.

———

The alchemist saved me, but I saved myself too. I wrote my story to be my own alchemist. I filled the chalk outline with my words. And months later, when that man who had hate fucked me reached out again, I said, "No. I'm done." And I was. When I next had a drink with Emily, I looked her in the eyes this time and said, "Safety is underrated." I was happy with the man who made me feel safe by then. I had needed to let go of the horror in order to make room for happiness.

There are different kinds of jumping. I could have jumped into the dark river to end my life, but I wanted to live.

I jumped out instead.

II

INSTITUTIONS

WHERE TO BOW TO
THE WILL OF THE MAJORITY

JEN KARETNICK

Collaged from the Pulitzer Prize–winning book
Advise and Consent, *by Allen Drury*

in schools, in clubs, in church classes and kindergartens
in battle and in politics
in a household that has as its head some noncommittal jest
in some little bar south of Market Street
in San Francisco and the Peninsula, the Coast and the Santa
                                                    Clara Valley
in a bank in Ogden with self-propelling elements
in this-is-the-way-it-is-done-because-this-is-the-way-we-
                                    have-always-done-it
in a fraternity or an early trial run
in a pleasantly self-sufficient land where eager girls make life
                                        happy for the football team
in ambition, which is the fashion of the executive committee
in exercising a habit
in the all-enveloping hypnosis of spring

WOMEN HAVE BEEN TRAINED

MARGE PIERCY

Women are trained to view their bodies
as assortments of parts to critique. Are
my breasts too small, too large, hairy,
low hanging, nipples too dark?

Is my belly too big, sagging, with stretch
marks, with scars? Are my hips too wide,
too narrow? My knees stick out too far.
My feet are too big, my toenails, yellow.

My nose must be replaced. Are my legs
too fat, too thin, bowlegged, knock-kneed,
not tan enough? Ashy? Chin too pointed,
too square, too weak, too masculine?

We are collections of complaints
taught us. The mirror is a jury.
Corporations thrive on manufactured
flaws: pricey creams to erase decades.

Weight watchers to make you model thin.
Bleach, go under the knife. Do Botox.
What law mandates the size of buttocks?
Who passed these rules we die by?

Revolution now! Crack the mirror.
Thrust out your ass, wriggle your hips.
Take long confident strides.
Rejoice in your *self* that's you.

THE PALLOR OF SURVIVAL

LAURE-ANNE BOSSELAAR

I don't know what happened to Judith Aaron,
placed in 1945 at the Mater Immaculata convent
in Brussels, after she was repatriated from Bergen-Belsen.

Judith who waited eleven years for some — *any* —
next of kin to claim her. No one ever came to the black
and brass door.

And we never saw her again after she turned
eighteen and left that morning, still in her convent
uniform, but the blouse open three buttons
down and the socks low on her white ankles.

She left on a sleety day in October, years after —
from under an infirmary bed I'd seen what the nuns
did to her when she confessed she masturbated:

bending her over, pulling down her panties
to ram the longest part of an ivory crucifix into her,
hissing: *HE is the Only One Who Can Come
Inside You — No One Else — You Hear?*

She didn't let out a sound, not a sigh:
the pallor of survival carved into her face
when she pulled her panties up again.

I think she made it: she was of the stone
statues are made from. And yet, I still search —
Judith, I can't stop searching — for signs

we made it: you, me and the others.
Signs I find in the smallest things: a flawless sky,
a leaf autumn turns, an open gate.

LIKE JUDITH SLAYING HOLOFERNES

PAUL TRAN

I know better than to leave the house
  without my good dress, my good knife

like Excalibur between my stone breasts.
  Mother would have me whipped,

would have me kneeling on rice until
  I shrilled so loud I rang the church

bells. *Didn't I tell you that elegance is our revenge,*
  that there are neither victims nor victors

but the bitch we envy in the end? I am that bitch.
  I am dogged. I am so damned

not even Death wanted me. He sent me back
  after you sacked my body

the way your armies sacked my village, stacked
  our headless idols in the river

where our children impaled themselves
  on rocks. I exit night and enter your tent

gilded in a bolt of stubborn sunlight. My sleeves
  already rolled up. I know they will say

I am a slut for showing this much skin, this
  irreverence for what is seen

when I ask to be seen. Look at me now: my thighs
    lift from your thighs, my mouth

spits poison into your mouth. You nasty beauty.
    I am no beast, but my blade

sliding clean through your thick neck
    while my maid keeps your blood off

me and my good dress will be a song
    the parish sings for centuries. Tell Mary.

Tell Eve. Tell Salome and David about me.
    Watch their faces, like yours, turn green.

ME TOO

NICOLE CALLIHAN

me too
said she
me too
said me
and i
said she
and me
said me
me too
me too
a cock
a shoe
me too
me too
in red
and blue
me too
me too
the cue
the dew
me too
said she
me too
said me
and me
and me
and me
and me
and me
and me
and me
too

GIRL AT THE WINDOW

RHONDA J. NELSON

At the bedroom door
he watches her stare
out the window, a dreamy
sentinel presiding over
the sailboats in the water
off Cadaqués. Singing
in a melodious language
that sounds like bells,
she's a tiny monolith,
a cherry tree with coiled
curls that he would willingly
tousle or comb.

He thinks any man who prefers
to look in her thirsty eyes
is mistaken. In that direction
lips could kiss or kill, a tongue
could prowl deep enough
to strangle. Face forward,
the rosebud blooms like
a thunderbolt to deliver
the world, leaves a man
floating in the ebb and flow
of afterbirth.

But from behind
she is motionless and safe.
He can anticipate the honey
of her buttocks like cake,

turning him into a vessel
of fanatical love, a borderline
between music and yesterday's
gardenia. He steps forward,
whispers to the back of her
neck . . . *If you respect our history*
I beg you, don't turn around.

REDEMPTION

BARBRA NIGHTINGALE

This is about
the spells cast on princesses,
the years they spend asleep.
How they awaken with a jolt
staring straight into the eyes
of some throbbing prince.

But this is not a fairy tale,
it is flesh and sweat.
There is sex and redemption,
violence and rapture.
There is moon and stars and wind,
there is a forest and a Big Bad Wolf.
But the woodcutter has a hard-on
and what he hacks is not for love.

There is thunder.
Storms polarize around me
like magnetic dust.
There is lightning and a vision.
There is the endless rain
that falls inside my heart.

HERE IS MY PUSSY

NICOLE CALLIHAN

It is not a particularly pretty pussy
a sometimes haggard pussy
but it is my pussy
it is my Prague in the spring pussy
my sweaty summer pussy
my two daughters wintered pussy
my in the classroom pussy
in the rainstorm pussy
longing for longing pussy
airplane bathroom pussy
fast train to DC pussy
little girl turned woman pussy
socked with shame pussy
white cotton underwear pussy
purple pantied black pantied pussy
red pantied no pantied pussy
Cackalacky and Connecticut pussy
Tampa pussy my pussy
and though I have pussy
footed through the barn pussy
footed through the city pussy
footed all the streets of Tulsa pussy
footed flat footed under willows pussy
footed on tiptoes to the river pussy
footed into my own marriage bed with pussy
willows blooming in my brain pussy
waxed and waned pussy
all mine yes my pussy
and yes I have wanted you to grab my pussy

have dreamed of you grabbing my pussy
have breathed the word pussy
into your ear have traced pussy
onto your back have written pussy
so many times it became other than pussy
became blossom or blame became pussy
again pussy again my pussy my pussy
to offer my pussy my pussy my pussy
to offer if I wish my pussy my pussy
all mine

HOW WE LIVED

EMMA TRELLES

2017, 2018, 2019 . . .

And sparrows unthread nests, bring their young nothing
And shadows best seen inside the pitch of a cave
And three men stabbed on a train because of courage
And jacarandas flick cinder and blacken the ground
And the harbor horn is a creature roping hulls to the reefs
And the reefs gleam with chrome and absence
And absence is welcome
The bullet is welcome
The malignant cell is welcome
The gray faces and their merciless tongues are welcome
And a father is reptilian in his regard. And a mother stitches
Her lips like a wound. And the wound smells of silence and its
    blaring
And a child lays hands on a mine. And a man swallows his lies
    without measure
And a woman is told she is less than him she is less than the bodies
    left
Behind, less than the unmade, the never-was, the dirt forgotten by
    the tracks
And I no longer care about the losses. I no longer care if the last
Bit of bark is stripped from the earth, if the starved possum survives
The road, whether my neighbor coughs blood while she drags off a
    red
Or the hand turning the knob means me harm. I no longer fear
The inexorable diagnosis, the oceans rising to such heights
In my dreams they are monstrous but we are all still running
Towards each other, in this latest hour, refusing to shutter our eyes.

SKY

MICHAEL HETTICH

Who took the chance to leave home with only
the clothes she was wearing, and someone else's name.

Who took the chance
to sleep without a blanket

in the litter-filled woods by the highway, in the rain:

Who closed her eyes
and slept while the delicate
animals sniffed her, and ravenous insects

by the millions slipped under her skin as she mumbled
a little in her dream. Did no one look for her?

Someone walks barefoot through the city in the dark,
a delicate woman with aching teeth
whose bones have been arranged like kindling, to burn.

We wake up to the smell of smoke and look up at the sky.

QUESTIONNAIRE
FOR TWO PUSSIES

DENISE DUHAMEL AND MAUREEN SEATON

When did you first realize you were a girl?

I was a year and a half when my brother was born early at four pounds. That's when I knew girls were bigger and strong and that I was one of them.

═

When I asked the priest if I could be an altar boy, he told me that I was a girl. I guess I knew before then, but that was the first time I internalized my girlhood and understood that some things would be forbidden to my kind.

Did you ever want to be a boy? If so, why?

The only time I ever wanted to be a boy was so I could play in Little League. I batted leftie and ran fast. Otherwise, there was no way. Boys were dumb. Tell them not to play on the railroad tracks and they did.

═

Never once did I wish I had balls, a beard, or a penis. Never once did I want to be in a fistfight or play football. Never once did I wish I could go to war.

How old were you the first time a stranger looked at you funny? Where were you? Where was he? Where were your parents?

I loved buying penny candy at Terry's—flying saucers made of wafers with tiny sweet beads rattling inside. Waxed lips and candy necklaces. Pixy Stix and orange Circus Peanuts. One day

Terry wasn't there and her husband leered at me from behind the register. I was seven. My parents had always thought Terry's was safe.

===

The first time I felt creeped out in public was in Manhattan. Maybe I was twelve. Some guy made an odd sound and looked at me funny. My parents didn't notice, and I was glad they didn't. I was embarrassed, like my slip was showing. (We wore slips in those days.)

Who is the first man you ever remember being leery of and what would you say to him now?

My eighth grade English teacher reeked of gin. He stumbled towards me sometimes, grinning. Once he asked me to stay after class, but I left pretty sure he'd forgotten. *What would I say to him now?* Because of you, I know the difference between an independent and dependent clause.

===

I'd rather not comment.

The time you were buying lubricant at the drugstore and that guy sidled up beside you, almost touching you, what did you do? What would you do now?

I never said a thing. I was screaming in a dream but no sound came out of my mouth. I was pushing 911, the numbers soft and blurring together, then the whole phone melting in my hand. Now I would zap him with my Axon Taser.

===

I'd like to say I would say something confrontative, but, actually, I'd probably just walk away quickly and leave the store, like I did then.

When did you go on your first real date?

In junior high, Tommy and I went bowling. Paul McCartney & Wings were singing "Maybe I'm Amazed" on the jukebox. It felt more than a bit sinful as we removed our footwear in front of each other, wiggled our toes, and slipped on our rented bowling shoes.

═══

Not until I was 16. My date told me women were manipulative and prima donnas and always got their way. That men didn't stand a chance when it came to being in the world with women. He was 16 too. I wondered what had happened to him to make him think those things. We only had that one date. Sometimes I wonder if he got married and if his wife survived.

Did you ever cry on a date because you were afraid?

I cried because he was swearing, looking at me instead of the road. I thought he would smash the car and kill us both.

═══

I never cried, but I was scared to death of this one guy who took me to a park and was all over me in a second. What the hell, I thought. What had I done wrong?

Did a guy ever tell you were frigid or a tease?

A couple of guys told me I was either frigid or a tease. Somehow, by some quirky happenstance of self-esteem and/or reality, I knew they were being ridiculous.

As I made out with a stranger at the party in Brookline, I changed my mind and thought I'd give my recent ex a second chance. When I pulled away and said I had to be going, the stranger said, "Cocktease bitch."

Did you ever have a kissing fantasy? A "grabbing" fantasy? A rape fantasy?

I have fantasized about kissing Sean Penn, Rosario Dawson, one of my bosses, and the mail carrier who told me he was planning to go to Argentina to practice his tango and fly-fishing. But never once did I fantasize that any of them rape me.

I never had fantasies about being forced to do anything I didn't want to do. Actually, I prefer reality to fantasy, that's why I write poems, not novels. I love this world. I love being a part of it, not someone else's idea of it or who I should be in it.

Any final comments?

We would simply note here that more than ten times a day we feel unsafe.

And that really pisses us off.

GB2G4

MICHAEL MACKIN O'MARA

After GM Hopkins

1. GRUMPY MANLEY CAT HOWLS

Lines written when my ex informed me
He'd given up crack for crystal meth

Glory be to God for faggot things—
    For T, for G, for crack, for AIDS;
        For throttled Haring outlines lynched
on gallery walls; for Basquiat corpses dancing, dancing;
    For "I love my dead gay son."— O glitter & be gay!
    For UB2 clean.

All things butch, femme, and in-between;
    "Whatever" to your washboards, your heroin chic?
        (Within heteronormative social construct shuns)
He drops a dub whose beauty is past tense:

        Fuck him-her-it-them

2. GRUMPY TRIES AGAIN

Glory be to God for fairy wings—
        For eyes of four-tone contact color, wow;
        For guy halter tops—¡Merci, Jean Paul!
Pink hot-pant overalls, button-down oxfords

Sleeves neatly rolled, well, folded, really;
  Hair: free, wild, and/or just-so.

All things counter-culture, urban, suburban, rural, fay;
  Whatever sparks spangled, feckless (brave?)
    With eye-water fountains & shaking hands;
They serve and shall whose beauty is begun:

  Selah, my adopted ones

3. AND AGAIN

Glory be to God for eff'd-up things—
  For, while bullets, eye-rolls shouldn't, yet they do;
  Snickering too. Another heart pierced .12-gauge.
O love-me, love-me, love-me—loathing;
  Chained no-never-no, lovesick, hacksawed. We-You
    think, thought, thunk, and still rage against

All things hateful from atom to atomic; from sea to shining
    —Don't get me started on man-infest destiny, whose
    Exterm of different, whose ill-gotten gains—
We muther-on in beauties, awestruck, strange:

Enough! For the love of God, peace (stfu)

ME TOO—THE FALL OF MAN

CYNTHIA NEELY

After the painting of Adam and Eve
by Peter Paul Rubens

Forgive me the need
to touch your breast,

though I did not ask
and you did not offer.

Then, its ripeness
leaned in so close.

Begging for it.

You were reaching
for something. What?

Something more?
Some knowledge

new and shining,
daring and delicious?

Or some idea beyond
what you already knew

your life would be
here with me.

Why should I not, then,
taste as well?

Would you get on your knees
to only pray?

That he punished me
too is so unfair.

I told you it was a secret.
I told you not to tell.

A BRIEF HISTORY IN PINK

MICHAEL MACKIN O'MARA

Dancing, They were dancing . . .

—ROBERT HASS

Pink is a triangle in Dachau, Pink is a 5K ribbon, Pink as a tongue
plunged into soft serve swirls, Pink as a sailor's sky, Pinked is
    pierced or
scalloped as by pinking shears, Pinks are *Dianthus plumarius's*
    nickname
their petals pink with pinked edges, Pink with possibility, Pink eye,
    Pink is
Barbie's signature color and cotton candy's, and flamingo's and the
roseate spoonbills by the lake which pinks briefly with the
    coming and
going light, and grapefruit though not always and if there is a way
    to tell
from the outside I don't know it, Pink as Piglet from Pooh and
BaRamEwe Babe content with *That'll do pig, that'll do*

Pink as a bubble gum balloon that I never blew, Pinkie rings,
    Pinky and
the Brain, Pink-o Liberal Commie Pink a.k.a. Rose or Salmon
    because real
men still tell me they don't, Ditto Pink when twice a year the priest
    dons
the prescribed vestments and also calls it anything but

Plastic Pink Flamingos, and Pink films, Pretty in, The Pink Panther,
    Pink
Narcissus, My Life in Pink,

Pink Floyd, Pink Elephants, Pink Cadillacs, Pink Albino Eyes, In
   the Pink,
Tickled Pink

(At some point, a point, please)

We knew you were that way (pink) when you were twelve . . .

Flaming Pink (as an oft-assertion), Pink like Pepto Bismol, Pink
   Lady: Gin
& Grenadine, Pink Champagne, Pink tutus and ballet toe shoes,
   Glinda
the Good Witch in Pink Tulle, Pink Pencil Erasers and all the
   undone

Pink Slips, Pink IZODS with their upturned collars, Pink hubs
   of a
hypodermic army, Pink Silence = Pink Death, Pink pistol
   whipped, tied
and left to weather starlight, Trans Pink shot, stabbed, pummeled

Pink Teens / Pink suicides, Dancing Pink, Scarlet Pink, Pink is a
   triangle,
Euclidean: Right, Oblique, Acute, Obtuse, Degenerate, a vector. In
   three

dimensions there are at least eight geometries, still in the infinite
multiverse Pinked. Bodies. Fall.

ONE IN FOUR

DAVID MCLOGHLIN

It has happened to a quarter of us
(us? Is that a community?)
twenty-five out of every one hundred
hung, hearts, spleen, and lungs
drawn, and everything is quartered,
memory split, hemisphered
like a dangerous rebel carcassed
and dispatched to the corners of the realm,
the Elizabethan, Cromwellian, Rome-subjugated
territory, so that no one will ever forget

or remember
twenty-five percent of this population
has been butchered.

The memories start to live back
through the limbic system
fragments of stained touch,
the flashbacks come
in the arms of real love.

Until it can be said,
until I can say, *me too*,
the crime will continue.
I join my voice to the silent chorus
to hold space for those who can't speak yet.
I speak, and I hold.
Hold the line.

THE PEACH ORCHARD

RITA DOVE

> *What the soul needs, it uses.*
>
> —JAMES HILLMAN

I say there is no memory of him
staining my palms and my mouth.
I walk about, no longer human—
something shameful, something
that can't move at all.

Women invented misery
but we don't understand it.
We hold it close and tell it
everything, cradle the ache
until it sleeps in and he's

gone, just like the wind
when the air stands still.
I'll step lightly
along the path between
the blossoming trees,

lightly over petals
drifting speechless and pale.
No other story could have
brought me here: this
stone floor. And branches

bank upon bank of them brimming
like a righteous mob, like

a ventriloquist humming,
his hand up
my spine . . . O these

trees, shedding all
over themselves.
Only a fool
would think such frenzy
beautiful.

RECIPE FOR RESISTANCE

JEN KARETNICK

Separate ten years of silence
from their aureate hearts.

Put those aside; you'll need that
embryonic blood later. Beat into

stiff peaks, then fold in a cup
of your boss's brand of sugar:

"Jews make good teachers,
because they all went to private

schools." Spice with, "If you come
bearing gifts, why are you still

wearing clothes?" and frost
with a story about the time

he flattened his hand like a spatula
against your thigh and slid it

up your skirt while his wife
sat unstirred on his other side.

You have tooth-picked a dozen
of these tidbits but worked there

because [. . .]. This is how
you cut and eat the cake

you have always wanted to bake.

KILLING

MIRIAM BIRD GREENBERG

How the blade was not sharp enough.
How a duck's neck is supple as a thick piece of rope.
How we squatted close to the damp dirt, nighttime
welling around our ankles. The old men
drunk by the gate had gone to their slanting houses;
no one was on the streets. We had a knife at least,
the kind you plunge into soil for cutting roots, blade
sharpened on both sides, but old, really. How I held her
wings bound against her struggle, my fingertips touching
at her breastbone. I had killed other animals
before, and once a broken-winged songbird
died of fright in my hands, but it is easy
to forget how something goes boneless
from fear. How the smell of shit rose from her warm body
after. Together we carried her in a burlap sack
through the dark streets, and blood bloomed
on the fabric between us and on the street.
She was a talisman through clusters of men,
only boys but larger, conducting transactions
not quietly, and no one spoke to us or met our eyes.
How, even once we plucked her clean and, safe,
someone set a pot to boil, traces of her smell
clung to our hands like strands of fog.
            How my pulse ran in my fingers
like the heartbeat of another thing.

TESTIMONY

DENISE DUHAMEL

After he tried to kiss me during his office hours,
I ducked and scrambled into the hall
wondering if I had imagined it. After he tried to kiss me,
he dismissed all of my poems in workshop
though I wondered if I was imagining that too.
Maybe I was indeed a mediocre writer. To get off
the TA waiting list, you were supposed to give the chair
a blowjob. I wish I were misremembering this. The two women
who received the teaching positions thought I was uptight
because I was brought up Catholic. I was drinking
back then—I confess—but no amount of wine
makes my testimony less true. It was the first time
I lived somewhere warm, even in the fall. I wondered
if I would have been safer in mittens and a coat. I wonder
what those two TAs remember of that time, if they feel shame
or rage or have somehow internalized it all.
I never spoke up. I had no language to do so—not even
in my poems which became conceptual and abstract. Instead,
I drove into the desert and posed as a cactus—
kind of like that yoga pose, though I didn't know
what yoga was all those years ago. I just wanted
thorns, those cholla spines that leapt out
when a predator came too close.

WORDS THAT KNOW THE SUN

YADDYRA PERALTA

One night, during the initial burst of #metoo sharing, my sister and I were on the phone talking about the Weinstein allegations. Some women went into specifics, perhaps not naming names but identifying the relationship: professor, boss, boyfriend, followed by a specific verb (pick one): touched, groped, raped—each detailing an unforgettable transgression and often a forced path into a new and lonely world. One I will never forget listed at least a dozen varied assaults, ranging from stranger touches on the street to date rape, all experienced on the fraught journey from childhood to adulthood.

Once my sister assured me she believed the women, I broke out into my own catalogue of abuse, all I couldn't share on social media. The cousin and stranger touches—at home and at the mall—the babysitter's son, the men in the NYC subway. The date rapes. She apologized for not knowing. She said she'd heard these things happen to a lot of women, "but I guess I've been lucky." I reminded her of the kid that exposed himself to her in seventh-grade health class and the teacher who shrugged when she told her telling her to "sit somewhere else." There was a momentary silence on the other end of that phone call like the sound of a world shifting.

As a poet and writer, I've written about many difficult subjects: mental illness, war, and exile. What one wants to say about traumatic experiences is often shaped or even muffled by the severity of the experience, societal or familial stigma, career-related repercussions, and/or very often, shame and victim-blaming turned inward. A predominant thought for me the last few months has been: why tackle this at all, especially in poetry?

Why not let sleeping dogs lie, as I've been taught to do by my own family?

Beyond the act of making poetry and taking back control of your narrative, voicing these experiences, even if only on the page—if one is ready to do so—speaking or writing about abuse, can be cathartic, can remove *some* stigma, not just for the writer, but for the reader too. This linking of two or more strangers or friends can create community. And communities are what are needed to effect changes small and large.

These days, I often think of Audre Lorde's "Coal," one of my early poetry loves. The poem is about many things, primarily Black identity, but a portion of it has always stuck with me because it reminds me of my work as a woman and as a poet and the often-difficult task of working with some words. The crucial part of the poem imagines words like venomous snakes, stuck in the speaker's throat, while others travel out through the mouth to meet the sun.

It has taken me a lifetime to process a progression of varying abuses that started at the age of four. And I've had to log years of practicing my craft before I felt ready to write about any of it. It's not yet automatic. I have a lot to consider as I work: Do I write the narrative as if it were someone else's story? Do I re-enter the consciousness that lived the experience? If I am triggering myself am I really healed? I don't know the answers to these questions. What I do know is that when I can do it—when I am ready to tackle such an experience in poetry or prose—the words that leave me and land on the page become someone else's once read out loud or published. I hope the work is a friend to someone who needs it, someone like me who once thought that she was in this alone.

BODY POLITIC

BOSCH JONES

I still love the drug
& how the fuck
    this unlikely president is one hell of a lot
    like me.

I crave a clean honeypot of pussy like a salver;
    so it must be true in doing the so called dirty work
that I am to kiss it, love on it, suck it up no matter what

goatish, overripe, or raw condition.
    Always it felt like I was doing something wrong.
    Well sugar, you probably were, but so what! Virginia said.

Dear friend, sometimes she held my head & with
hands on my ears would guide me gently down
    décolletage way, saying
        cummere honey have some boobie!

Please give my face what you think
    it needs, a good rub & press against
a cleft; the constitution

balloons with a loosed indifference tricky, so you could
pop it in the warmer later, maybe I guess, if you want.

Aching watch, it cleaves to my forearms & fingertips.
Starts up the inside & works its way out like a swallow.

Is this not the best thing I could possibly be
right now, world slipping into the sword's mighty mug.

Call it *crazy chick shit* or whatever you want, it is important
when considering her losses in elections. It appears

systemic inheritance proves some ladies are lady
killer of

These culprits they wanna paw allover
            & live like slobovians—well then let them
        do it to themselves.
& you know what she said?
            She said like this:
        she say
        your brain she NEED washin!

SPEAKER OF THE HOUSE

SAPPHIRE

Speaker of the House
second in line for the presidency—
someone knocks off the president,
the VP has a heart attack & voila!
You're it. A rise. You rose.
We watched bewildered, angry & confused—
Remembering when your hair was a thick dark gleam
your chunky body a slab of marbled meat, your judgment
leading us on, on the mat, in our lives
to the championship—
Top of the world—small town boys, Winners.
You moved on, left us behind
                    Illinois House of Representatives
              United States House of Representatives
       51st Speaker of the United States House of Representatives
I have difficulty believing someone will love me,
that my body is even worth taking care of.
I don't even feel good unless I'm on something.
It seems like I'll never be anything again—
the last I was anything was with you.
Now I'm nothing watching you on TV
hearing about what you own, where you've been,
the good you've done, what a down home regular
guy you are while I feel like a piece of shit.
Pop pop poppers white lines disappear my face
in the mirror. I don't search out the other boys, men now
I feel creepy I feel they might feel
I was weird gay or something. They might remember

excitement I felt warmth rising looking
at other boys, no looking allowed, I bring my eyes down.
I'm older now decades pass—I'm afraid.
Afraid at interviews, my heart fluttering like my
eighty-year-old aunt, my palms drip
"Tell us, what are your strengths? What were the major challenges
of your last job?" Major accomplishments? I can't think of anything
except how sweat is gushing from my armpits and through
my white shirt fouling my blue suit.
Last job? I lost that job, the job before that too
Absent, absences, attitude, missing in action
I like to ride motorcycles, crank, speed go fast
"I'm punctual," I say out loud, "and a hard worker."
When I choose to show up. Something I've accomplished?
Something good—when I was a kid I helped
Hastert, Dennis Hastert. I was his assistant,
too small to wrestle, I was still an integral part
of the team, helping them, helping him. We won
the state championship. Do you know what it feels like
to be number one, to be a boy from a small town or broken
home or poor or black or "different"—
What do you have except that? You know what that feels like?
Teachers, girls, boys, cashier at Walmart's, guy at the gas station
waitress at IHOP—everybody in town!
You know what it feels like to be part of something, to be
Number one.
Just one time, he said, just do this for me one time.
It was god asking, the voice leading me from
my Pop's life, the one he fell down on, the assembly
line that kept moving even though he had stopped.
Say your prayers, work hard, believe in god
things will fall in place. You rise. This is America
where a man can go from being a small town coach
to Speaker of the House, can amass wealth wife kids property

shake hands with heads of state, hobnob with household names,
America, where you're not born into anything
that you can't work your way out of.
You work hard, he told us, what you practice you become.
When you walk out on that mat—you against your opponent—
you're not as good as he is, you're better!
He talked to me like that even though I was too small
to wrestle and the equivalent of a bat boy
he treated me like part of the team even though
I was toting towels and water. But you know something
I never rose. It was like something was always missing.
The way he looked at me froze my blood
plagued the lining of my stomach.
His big belly, after-shavie smell mixed with sweat.
"I need you," he said.
My hormones surged, boys looked at me
and I looked back—so that's why
he did what he did to me—I was gay.
I couldn't keep up in college, one man hit me
one man raped me, I wanted to but didn't use condoms
no one did, only one guy, a black guy, did.
Strange you hear so much about them—bad like I'm bad
my desires bad, my body bad, wipes me out
disappears me little death after little death
Love should give me *life*
but it doesn't. I don't tell anyone
I'm like a woman with a past
trying to get some fool to marry her—
white clean Christian boy, not what I feel like
I seek Tops pain: GWM seeks—what was I seeking?
What I got was AIDS, blank faces who wouldn't hire me
I began to seek a little lower, minimum wage. No one ever
                            expected anything of me anyway. I
had never really been on the team,

a servant really, and lucky to be that, he told me. Bastard!
What a way he had with us, with words, with the world!
Speaker of the House—top of the world!
While I drifted down toward the bottom which kept descending.
One day I Tell.
I tell my sister what you did to me.
Ahh! Finally the missing piece, she understands,
wants to fix it. But it's too late.
I die of AIDS and you keep rising.
Where I could live is in your memory
But you amnesiac don't remember a thing.
No, I'm erased silenced slammed to the mat.
But a bell rings, it's not over—another round
I'm dead but I start to rise in whispers, innuendoes, finally
federal investigators. And I hear the house
Your house—
The House of Hastert is coming down.

"IT'S JUST WORDS, FOLKS. IT'S JUST WORDS."

—DONALD TRUMP, OCTOBER 9, 2016

DENISE DUHAMEL

'Twas nasty, and the slithy bimbos
    Did gyre and whine in the pageant:
All piggy were the gold diggers,
    And the moms who breastfed in public.

"Beware the pussy, my sons!
    The jaws that bite, the claws that catch!
Beware those plastic surgery tits, and shun
    Any frump who won't put out!"

Trump took his vorpal sword in hand:
    Long time *Maxim* subscriber, he tugged—
Then rested he in his Tumtum tower,
    And stood awhile in thought.

And, as in lustful thought he stood,
    He saw Hillary, with eyes of flame.
Still, Trump touched his wood,
    And burbled as he came!

One, two! One, two! And through and through
    His vorpal blade went snicker-snack!
We thought his presidential chances dead,
    Yet Trump came galumphing back.

"Only I have slain the democrats!
    Come to my arms, underage girls!
O frabjous day! How much do you weigh?"
    We watched Trump's flag unfurl.

///

IMPOSTERS

GROPE

JESSICA CUELLO

The touch I wished for
floated in the ether,
brushing my face gently
in a distant future.

The hand I wanted
to remain on my back
the one time
my mom touched me

tenderly
is why I said nothing
when he pushed me
against the metal door

where the cold air blew in
from the loading dock.
It was the janitor's door.
His hand, lean as a hanger,

all bone, went to my chest,
then neck.
He was so close
I saw the shiny inside

of his ear, the hairs
emerging from his scalp.
Startled into second-sight,
I glimpsed his home,

the people there old irons
like the people in mine,
which is why he grabbed me:
untouched recognizes

untouched.
For months after, he stared
at me like I was a sister
bearing his home secrets

as if I would tell
as if I would ever unload
the corners of myself
into the ears of school

but I did give him
the evil eye
and dump used lunch trays
in his locker.

AT LEAST I DIDN'T RAPE YOU

CARIDAD MORO

The wine we shared did it. You leaned in
and offered me some killer advice

because we both turned to look at the brunette
who passed our table on the way to the bathroom—

*Since you're into chicks, you might as well
think as if you had a dick.*

*You have the power of preemptive strike.
Just follow her into the john,*

*wait until she leaves the stall, then push her
against the wall. Take what you want.*

*Most guys won't admit it,
but if we had our way we'd knock you down,*

*spread your legs and plunge ourselves
into what we want.*

I consoled myself with all that could have been worse
than discovering you were the kind of man

my father would have understood, the kind
of man who considered a woman nothing

more than split and cleft, orifice, cavity,
study in absence, a maw, a void;

worse than my girlhood, litany of less than
Papi hammered into my head

the worst of his words exhumed, corroborated
by the pick and spade of your confession—

Hija, a key that opens many locks is a master key;
don't be the slut with the busted deadbolt.

I'd rather kill you,
than let you become a whore.

At least I didn't rape you.
Don't you know how lucky you are?

COCOA BEACH

TERRY GODBEY

I hadn't realized a man could slice me open.
Mid-sentence I cut my boyfriend off, started walking
home along the causeway. Leggy and tanned,
I didn't have to put up with a damn thing.

Mid-sentence I cut my boyfriend off, started walking
in the dark. His car pulled up. *Get in.*
I didn't have to put up with a damn thing,
thrust my chin out and kept walking. *Get lost!*

In the dark another car pulled up.
A beater with three men. *Want a ride?*
I thrust my chin out and kept walking. *No thanks.*
The air swelled with the smell of ripening pears.

A beater with three men. *Want a ride?*
They eased out of the car. I backed away.
The air swelled with the smell of ripening pears.
I looked for cover — marsh grass, river.

They eased out of the car. I backed away.
Muck soaked my sandals, wicked up my jeans.
I looked for cover — marsh grass, river,
forgot my fear of gators and water moccasins.

Muck soaked my sandals, wicked up my jeans.
Boots snapped the gravel. *Where is the little bitch?*
I forgot my fear of gators and water moccasins.
A voice nearby: *Anyone got a flashlight?*

Boots snapped the gravel. *Where is the little bitch?*
I even wished my boyfriend would come back.
A voice nearby: *Forget the flashlight! Let's go.*
I couldn't move, afraid it was a trick.

I even wished my boyfriend would come back.
Car lights blurred and bled along the causeway.
I couldn't move, afraid it was a trick,
then stumbled to my feet and started walking.

Car lights blurred and bled along the causeway.
I stayed far off the road, watched for brake lights,
stumbled over fire ant hills. I kept walking.
I might not ever leave my house again.

I stayed far off the road, watched for brake lights
all along the causeway. Leggy and tanned,
I might not ever leave my house again.
I hadn't realized a man could slice me open.

CRANK CALLER

NIKKI MOUSTAKI

In 1982, the most advanced piece of communication technology in my house was a clunky beige 1970s princess phone. I was twelve years old, an only child and latchkey kid, and the phone was my primary source of amusement. I was on it a lot, though my parents had warned me not to monopolize the line. We didn't have call waiting then because no one did—it wouldn't be available for several years—and my parents liked to call me from their jobs as car salespeople to ensure that I hadn't burned the house down and that I was doing my homework. If I was on the phone, they'd get a busy signal.

I had a small black-and-white TV set in my room, but it only received eight channels, two of which featured evangelical preachers. To change the channel, I had to get up and use a pair of needle-nose pliers because the knob had broken off. I was watching *General Hospital* one day after school, inches from the screen, pulsing with an unbridled love for John Stamos, when the phone rang.

A man was panting at the other end of the line, a moist, breathy voice, practically a gurgle. At my age, I knew all the "dirty" words the crank caller was breathing into the phone, but I hadn't heard them all in one run-on sentence before, and never directed at me.

The crank caller whispered all the pornographic things he wanted to do to me. "I'm going to get you," he groaned. "I'm going to get you."

He sounded like an adult and had obviously dialed the wrong number. I hung up, shuddered, and turned back to watch John Stamos with his silky feathered hair and tight pants.

The phone rang again.

"I'm going to suck your cunt," the caller breathed. "I'm going to lick your pussy I'm going to fuck you I'm going to bend you over and do your ass I'm going to get you."

"You have the wrong number," I said before slamming the receiver into its cradle.

The phone rang again. It was him, panting, breathless. "I'm going to get you, *Nicole*."

He'd said my name. This call *was* for me.

I sprung up and ran around the house, making sure that the doors and windows were locked. The phone was ringing, ringing, ringing. I felt clammy and scared. We didn't have an answering machine. The phone insisted to be answered. I picked it up. Maybe it was my parents or grandfather, who often called me in the afternoons. I couldn't ignore it.

A long, hissing breath filled the other end of the line. "I'm going to lick your sweet cunt," the crank caller said.

I pressed the hang up button and called my mom at the Subaru dealership.

"What time are you coming home?" I asked her, trying to calm my quavering voice.

"The usual," she said. "Everything okay?"

I looked at the clock. It would be hours before either of my parents walked through the door. I wanted to tell her about the crank caller, but I couldn't say his words out loud. I'd be grounded if I cursed. Being honest wasn't worth the trouble, anyway. My parents' philosophy seemed to be that everything that happened to me was my fault, even if I was the victim. If I became sick, it was because of something I ate or from sitting too close to a sick kid in class. If I was picked on at school, I must have done something to attract the bully's attention.

"Everything's fine," I said.

The phone rang again the moment I hung it up. "I'm going to fuck your little pussy," the crank caller whispered. I slammed down the phone. My hand trembled as I pulled the receiver off the cradle and only replaced it when I heard my father's Volkswagen pull into the driveway.

I had put the crank caller out of my mind by dinnertime. Crank calls were a regular part of life before phone technology erased anonymity. My friends and I crank called random strangers from the White Pages all the time. We couldn't get caught. Radio stations were a hot target. We stayed up late at sleepovers and called talk shows, attempting to sound like adults, trying to stifle our laughter before spilling a litany of curse words, hoping they wouldn't hang up before our voices went over the airwaves.

The next afternoon, the phone rang in the middle of my John Stamos fix.

"I'm going to lick your little pussy I'm going to suck your cunt I'm going to fuck your ass I'm going to get you, *Nicole*," the crank caller exhaled into the phone in one long breath.

I hung up. He called again. I hung up. He called again.

He called the next day, too. He called every day until my parents came home from work. Every day the same words and phrases, the same gurgling voice on repeat.

"Someone keeps calling and hanging up," my mom said to me one day. "Must be one of your little friends. Maybe it's a boy? Do you have a boyfriend I don't know about?"

No, I didn't have a boyfriend.

The crank caller was relentless. He called ten times a day, sometimes twenty or more, though he rarely called on weekends. The only reprieve I had was when we went on vacation.

I didn't tell anyone. I was ashamed somehow. When my parents asked me why I'd started sleeping with the lights on, I said I slept better that way. When they went to bed, I snuck downstairs every night to make sure the doors and windows were locked.

By the time I was fourteen I wasn't as scared of him anymore. He'd told me hundreds of times that he was going get me, but I still hadn't been got.

"Fuck you!" I shouted into the phone when he called. "Don't call here again!"

When I cursed at him, he called more.

His calls became part of my daily routine: Wake up, eat breakfast, go to school, come home from school, field between two and twenty crank calls, take phone off hook, do homework, answer more crank calls, eat dinner, watch TV, go to bed. I was a virgin, but I felt callous about the thought of someone performing sexual acts on me. I'd had the idea repeated into my ear a thousand times. Was it really a big deal?

As the years went on, the crank caller became bolder and started calling when my parents were home. They'd ask from downstairs who was on the phone and I'd answer that it was a wrong number.

When I was seventeen, the phone company started offering voice mail, caller ID, and a new service, last-call return—better known as *69—for just under ten dollars a month. When the *69 buttons were pressed, the phone would dial back the last person who called. I begged my mom to add these features to our line.

"The phone is fine the way it is," she'd said. "If someone wants to reach us, they'll just have to call back. It's too expensive, anyway."

The crank caller kept calling.

When I was eighteen, my parents told me we were moving. I was elated. At that time, moving meant that you'd get a new phone number. By then I figured that the crank caller had called me over six thousand times. I'd had enough.

My first week in the new house with the new phone number—he called. This was my first and only clue about his identity. It had to be someone I knew.

I heard from the crank caller less in my later teenage years because I was out of the house more, but when I was home he managed to reach me. Sometimes I rolled my eyes and hung up. Sometimes I got angry. He was annoying and disgusting. I desperately wanted this to stop.

When I was twenty and in college, living at home to save money, still regularly listening to this man's heavy breathing and rote sexual desires, the phone company decided to make its call waiting package—complete with *69—available for free to all of its customers.

My happiness could not be measured.

I sat by the phone. It rang a lot—but it was never him. I called in sick from my part-time job at the pet store to wait by the phone, only to sit in hours of silence. This man had terrorized me for over eight years. I figured that he'd called me more than ten thousand times since I was twelve years old. Couldn't he call just once more?

A week later, home alone, I absently answered the phone. "I'm going to lick your pussy I'm going to suck your cunt I'm going to fuck your ass I'm going to get you," he panted. I smiled and gently hung up.

Then I dialed *69. A voice came on the line after two rings.

"Hello, this is Michael from Michael's Jewelry, how can I help you?" a man said in a clear, pleasant voice.

I felt sick and euphoric at the same time. My face flushed and the world felt hot and plastic, the phone in my hand barely there. I knew this man. Michael from Michael's Jewelry was an old family friend. He'd sat across the dinner table from me a hundred times. I'd known him since I was a little girl. He even spent the night on our couch, twenty feet away from the door to my room, when my grandmother had passed away.

I lost my voice for a moment.

"Hello?" he said. "Can I help you?"

"I know who you are," I growled, finding my voice again. "If you *ever* call me again I'm going to tell on you. You have *one* chance."

He hung up.

Not only did Michael from Michael's Jewelry never call me again, he never looked at me again either. I hated him more for it. He'd sit at our table, eating my mother's pot roast and telling jokes as I seethed. I still couldn't bring myself to tell anyone what he'd done. He'd gotten away with scaring a young girl, sexual advances toward a child, wasting years of my time, forcing the sounds of a ringing phone and his voice in my dreams.

Years later, when my grandfather told me that the jewelry store had been robbed and Michael was beaten so badly that the thieves had broken his nose, I finally felt satisfied that our long conversation was over.

SWEET SIXTEEN

TERRY GODBEY

I was carrying on about my milestone.
Next door, Rita was carrying on
with my best friend's father.

No one blamed her. Rita's husband,
Big Ralph, with flying saucer ears,
a chin that pooled like a doughnut,
never let Rita have any money.
She scrubbed floors at the base hospital,
took care of whiny Little Ralph,
owned exactly two housedresses, both plaid,
of discordant, spectacular hues.

I bounced out of bed on my birthday
to miniskirts and Stones records,
a reprieve from housework
and mushroom steak for dinner.
Mom and I left the dishes to soak,
joined Rita outdoors in the lawn chairs.
Terry's 16 years old today, my mother announced.

Big Ralph, greasy and bent over the hood
of his old Chevy, dragged over a webbed chair,
squeezed into it and pulled me onto his lap.
Sweet sixteen and never been kissed,
he shouted, whacking my bottom
with one meaty paw,
restraining me with the other.

Stop, I yelled.
STOP!
I slapped and kicked and glimpsed
through his thick, hairy ankles
the upside-down arrival of friends, neighbors.
I'm gonna spank you one time, he said, panting,
for . . . every . . . year!

I was sorry to be so old, sorrier still
to be so young. My mind spun
with wishes, and not the birthday-candle kind:
*May the base commander rip the stripes
off your massive sleeves, may Little Ralph grow
to hate you as much as I do, may Rita's lovers
line the block.* When he finished, I scrambled
to my feet, tried not to cry, snarled *That hurt!*
Aw, honey, he said, still smiling,
if that's the worst pain you ever know . . .

Rita sighed.
My mother lit another cigarette.

SUMMER JOB

NY, CIRCA 1997

CATHERINE ESPOSITO PRESCOTT

Twenty years after I was pinned to the backseat of that preppy
    boy's car,

with a head heavy from working a 10-hour shift and from
    whatever he gave

me to drink (smallest illegal offering, what again was I worth?),
    I thought

of the apocryphal story of the mother who lifts a truck off of
    her baby to save him.

When I came to and said *not yet,* and he wouldn't stop, I heaved
    this boy

off of me with everything I had—a knee jab to the crotch, two
    determined

arms, hands which had never made a fist working overtime. *You
    fucking bitch,*

he said as he caught his breath. *I'll walk,* I whispered. I don't
    know why I didn't

run that mile back to town, why I sat in the front seat waiting
    for him to calm

down, why I believed he would do the right thing. Because he
stopped fighting?

Fact: We parked by the beach. Moonlight lifted over the bay,
sparkled on beach sand.

Fact: He tried to rape me, and I fought myself free. If babies are
extensions

of their mothers, of course she knows how to move two tons.
It's not the first time

she summoned every muscle in her body and every cunning
force to save herself.

PUERTO RICAN PUSSY

ANA MENÉNDEZ

"I don't like Puerto Rican pussy,"
the older boy said to a friend.
He was talking about a girl with a crush:
So, yes, he was talking about me.

This was 1982, in a private
Christian school in the South
Where daily Jesus and Satan battled it out
For our pliant, immortal souls.

And I was confused because
It didn't seem so godly, what he said
Though he was close to the minister
And seemed fed on God's beauty.

And I was puzzled, it's true, not understanding
All the words he used or the reason
For his hasty denial, three words
The apostle Peter surely never uttered
          Puerto Rican Pussy.

But I was twelve years old
And my bewilderment mainly sprang
From the fact that I was
Cuban and not a cat.

UP FOR GRABS

MAGGIE SMITH

"Boys chase girls" is the game I most remember playing during elementary school recess. It was wild and thrilling to sprint across the blacktop and through the ball field, and we ran like hell because who knew what the boys might do to us if they caught us? Or we ran like hell because we knew. Even as children, we understood what could happen to girls who were caught.

I can't remember a time before I thought of my body—my "private parts" in particular—as something to hide, something that could be taken from me. I was seven, eight, nine, and I couldn't hang upside down on the monkey bars if I was wearing a dress. On the swings I had to tuck the skirt between my legs and underneath me.

I can't remember anything before the constellation of shame, power, and fear: to accept that the body is something to be ashamed of is to believe that it has secret power; to believe in your body's power and to hide it is to be frightened of its power.

I wonder now, thirty-some years removed from that playground game, at what age girls learn to be afraid in their own bodies—*of* their own bodies? At what age do girls learn to make themselves smaller, less visible, for their own safety? When do girls learn that to be seen is to be *up for grabs*?

I was twelve, in seventh grade, and the same boy kept snapping my bra in the hallway. I was always fussing with my shirt, worried my bra straps were showing. I was worried someone would see me slip a tampon into my sleeve before I asked for the hall pass. I ran-walked to the restroom, worried I'd bled through my jeans.

I was twelve and my body troubled my mind.

I remember having to change before I went to a birthday party: according to my mother, my skirt was too short and too tight. I wore jeans and a Guess tee shirt—it was 1989—but stuffed the skirt into my bag. At the party I changed into the black tube skirt my mother was right about. I know she was right about it, and I wore it anyway.

I was twelve and I couldn't decide if I wanted to be seen or invisible.

Even then I sensed that invisibility is safety. And that to be noticed, to be desired, is dangerous. Already the boys came closer, testing, trying to see what they could get away with. Their bodies were becoming strange to them, too. They wanted. And we girls could smell their wanting from across a room. The air was thick with it. And likely, the air was thick with our wanting, too. With our desire and fear and shame.

=

I was fifteen when I lost my virginity to a mediocre boy who attended a local private school. I was impressed enough by him— his swoop of brown hair, his friends who were all strangers to me—to overlook the fact that he was an asshole, that he didn't care at all about me, and that I was certainly not the only one he was with. But it was hard to say no. It was so much easier to be small and silent, practically invisible. Easier to go somewhere else in my mind and stay there as long as I needed to.

I still remember almost nothing about that night.

=

Even in my forties, I'm vulnerable, a target. Aren't we still playing "boys chase girls," except now, it is not a game? When I know I'll be walking alone at night, it crosses my mind to wear shoes I could run in. I know I need to keep my eyes open, my ears open. I need to have my hands free. I need to be able to reach my phone. Even in my car, I'm vigilant. I lock the doors as soon as I climb inside and keep them locked. I don't roll down the windows for strangers.

Maybe this sounds paranoid, especially to men, but I think women know: this is what it is to feel like prey. We are vigilant about our bodies because we know—we have always known, for as long as we can remember—that we are on the menu, up for grabs. We know that someone could snatch us right off the street, or force their way into our cars or apartments.

More likely, the person who hurts us will not be a stranger; it will be someone we know and trust. Often someone we love.

=

Now I am the mother of a daughter and a son. My children go to elementary school a few blocks from our house, and sometimes I'm out walking the dog or running errands when they are at recess. I walk or drive by the school and see the kids, running, throwing a football in the muddy field, playing tetherball, climbing on the big blue dome. And if I remember what my children are wearing that day, I search for them in the sea of shirts and jackets.

I walk my children to school each day and I go back in the afternoon to walk them home. I tell them not to talk to strangers, not to approach cars. They want to know why people kidnap kids. They ask, *What do they want a kid for? What do they do with them? Do they give them back?*

What I can't bring myself to tell them, because I can hardly tell myself, is that they are more likely to be hurt by someone they know than a stranger in a panel van lying about a puppy. I tell them not to go into anyone's house unless I say it's all right.

I don't let them have playdates or sleepovers unless I know the parents well. And still, I cannot guarantee their safety any more than I can guarantee my own. This is the world we live in.

≡

I have a daughter: How do I teach her to love and respect her body?

I have a son: How do I teach him to love and respect his body, and to respect the bodies of others?

I tell my children that they don't have to hug anyone, not ever. They never have to sit on anyone's lap. They can high-five if they want, or fist-bump, or shake hands, or just use their words: *hello, thank you, goodbye*. They can keep their distance. I tell them, *Even if someone is your friend or cousin or aunt or grandpa, if you don't want to be touched, that's okay. Even if that person is me, that's okay.* I say, *Your body is your own, all yours, and you decide.*

Though I haven't yet used the word *consent*, I tell my children to ask if a friend wants a hug, because they might not. I tell them to run all they want, but no grabbing. I say, *Their bodies are their own, all theirs, and they decide.*

≡

My daughter has long, dark blonde hair, like honey. She has big blue eyes and a dimple in her right cheek. She is ten years old, on the cusp of so many changes. Now when she gets undressed and puts on her pajamas at night, she turns her back to me. She showers with the door closed, careful not to be seen unclothed.

I can admit this: when she was just a toddler, I worried about her blue eyes and blonde hair. I worried about the dimple when she smiles. When people would see her, they'd say things like, *Oh, you're in trouble with that one.* They'd say, *That one's going to be a looker*, and *She's going to break some hearts.* The way we sexualize children is disturbing—and not only girls. How many *Mommy's little heartbreaker* onesies did my son receive when he was born?

But the fact remains: I fear for my beautiful daughter in ways I do not fear for my beautiful son. How do I protect her without telling her she's prey, up for grabs? How can I keep her safe but not make her fear the world she lives in—or the *body* she lives in?

I don't have an answer because I don't think there is an answer. We do our best. I do my best to balance my own fear as a woman and my desire—and right—to move freely in this world. I do my best to keep my children safe without painting the world as a dark and dangerous place.

If my daughter must fear, if she must be wary and vigilant, at least let her be unashamed. At least let her know her power. And let her run. Let her run like hell, and let her not be caught.

ME TOO LIMERICK
WITH SIX DRUMBEATS

BRENDA HILLMAN

When i was young & sweet (er)   (uh)

He made a pass at me   (uh-uh)

When i said no

My poem didn't go   (uh)

In his anthology   (uh-uh)

WHAT SHE TOLD ME

SILVIA CURBELO

She couldn't stay, the great
house seemed so still,
and when he said her name
the word rose up inside her
ancient and familiar as
any war-torn street.

It wasn't right, but still
she had her reasons, and when
he moved against her
she felt a dark wheel
turning, the clock pushing
its dozen severed hands.

She wasn't young, there were
no fences left to climb,
and when he touched her face
there was no mistaking
the way the curtains parted onto
the deep, violent green of the lawn.

The sky changed colors the way
a sentence changes everything.
Silence can be a window
or a word. And when he said
her name she felt the shadow
of that voice fill every room.

PINK UNDERPANTS

MOLLY PEACOCK

We're both fully clothed in this romance where
the springy leg elastic is for keeping
the mons tucked neat inside the underpants
even when my skirt starts creeping up:
him atop me on my college sophomore bed.
Grad student with elegant fingers.
His long, pale learnèd index finger that
usually pointed to verse lines with embedded
symbols, now with its same swift expertise
suddenly flips the elastic aside—
its guardian SNAP! all confused when teased
away into silence.   And then he is inside.

How does he manage it when my legs are closed?
His hero's face enhanced by its flaw—
a slanted lip scar—superimposed on
my will, frozen . . . But watching the awed
agony of his pleasure unfreezes
my defenses, and my legs squeeze him out. Out-
raged, he leaves. We don't speak that year. All fine.
I bury him like a symbol in a line.

A pink elasticity snaps back when,
trusted Molly is appointed Junior Rep,
the thing I'd buried brought suddenly back
at the Dorm Committee Meeting. *He's* back,
applying for our Resident's job. Leap—
but so internal the leap seems *still*,

confused, until—a cool swift reason
parts my lips with enthusiasm for
another applicant as persuasive
as something that stands for something else. Rip,
slight, like nylon in a romance grip
as his blue-black elegant signature
is tied off in the ligature of the No pile,
collared beneath a metal clip.
                              Nothing
was clear or pure or direct.

EL AMERICANO IN THE MIRROR

RICHARD BLANCO

Maybe you don't remember, or don't want to, or
maybe, like me, you've never been able to forget:
May 1979, fifth grade recess, I grabbed your collar
shoved you up against the wall behind the chapel,
called you a sissy-ass *americano* to your face, then
punched you—hard as I could. Maybe you still live,
as I do, with the awful crack of my knuckles' slam
on your jaw, and the grim memory of your lip split.

Why didn't you punch me back? That would've hurt
less than the jab of your blue eyes dulled with pain—
how you let your body wilt, lean into me, and we
walked arm-in-arm to the boys' room, washed off
the blood and dirt. Is that how you remember it?
What you can't remember is what I thought when
our gazes locked in the mirror and I wanted to say:
I'm sorry, perhaps *I love you*, perhaps even kiss you.

Or did you feel it, too? At that instant did we both
somehow understand what I'm only now capable
of putting into these words: that I didn't hate you—
I envied you—the *americano* sissy I wanted to be
with sheer skin, dainty freckles, the bold consonants
of your English name, your perfectly starched shirts,
pleated pants, that showy *Happy Days* lunchbox,
your A-plus spelling quizzes that I barely passed.

Why didn't you snitch on me? I don't remember
who told Sister Magdalene, but I can't forget how

she wrung my ears until I cried for you, dragged me
to the back of the room, made me stand two hours
every day that week praying the rosary to think hard
about my sins. And I did, I have for thirty-eight years,
Derek. Whether you don't remember, don't want to,
or never forgot: forgive me, so I might forgive myself.

THRESHOLD

DENISE DUHAMEL AND JULIE MARIE WADE

It was autumn in the Midwest. I won't get more specific than that. I was thirty, give or take. I had lived with my partner for many years. In fact, I could hear her laughing—her sincere laugh—in the next room with this man's wife. "Shall we?" I said, rising. He rose also, nodded, then reached over and cupped my ass with his hand, gave it a firm squeeze, waited. A voice in my head said, Call out to his wife! Expose him! Another said, reminiscent of my mother, Knee him in the groin! He was grinning by then. He was daring me to do something he knew I wouldn't do. But the worst part was—the voice in my head that was louder than all the others said—Why would he grab my ass when his wife has a much better body?

===

A colleague from another department pinched my ass after I'd forgotten his name. He was an earnest kind of guy, with no signs of outward machismo. I pretended it didn't happen. I pretended it was a bee sting. I pretended I was kidding around. Of course I know your name. My colleague's wife was a knitter. Though I'd never met her, he once made a big deal of the scarf she'd made him. I pretended I'd backed into one of her needles. I avoided him for a long time after, staying on a different side of the room if we had to be in the same one. I thought maybe he had a crush. But a year later he said, "I owe you an apology for that goosing. It's just that I hate being invisible and—well, frankly—you remind me of my sister."

WHEN A WHITE MAN ATTEMPTS TO STEAL YOUR SOUL

HARI ZIYAD

He is always unattractive. Even though I might have found him cute on the street, things are different in the steam room of the gym. Something about the way he hides behind the vapor brings to mind a dementor, or the fog I imagine always follows the Reaper. Or maybe it's the feeling that, as he licks his lips, the sweat escaping through my pores carries out with it whatever keeps my heart beating. The link he maintains between his eyes and the parts of my body he desires becomes unshakeable. I am never the water guiding this cruise—just the ship, overturned. They say they are made of the same thing, but being stuck in the fog of this tiny wooden room is not what I envisioned a cloud to be like. I've seen far too many pictures of an old white god laying across a fluffy nimbus, and I suppose I haven't fully stopped believing in Him because I keep expecting this cloud of steam to carry me up toward a heaven where my body is mine. But Black queer boys don't get to be like those gods, and inhaling the blistering mist only makes me feel weak.

I have heard that you should leave the steam room when you begin to feel light-headed; that's when you know the vaporized air is failing to give your blood the oxygen it requires. But as I stare down the white man cruising for Black boys who walk into this dimly lit crate, the dizziness happens too fast to acquiesce to sage advice. For my muscles to relax after any workout worth its salt and the sweat that offered it as sacrifice, I'd have to stay inside a little longer. So I linger through the disorientation for just a few more moments. But I cannot relax when the "no" of my death stare only excites him. When my death excites him. When my soul leaving my body excites him.

Soul-stealing doesn't have to happen via touch. He doesn't even show me anything beneath his towel at first, though the hand the towel covers in his lap moves in slow rhythms. The critical line, located in some vague place between inappropriate annoyance and "legitimate rape," is never crossed. Any violation of my body is documentable only in my mind, and may have only occurred there, too. I might just be a bitter Black boy who hates white men. There is no law against white men stealing souls. And I have never written anything into law.

Instead, I write these stories about sitting through my death, the death that is being Black and queer in this world, over and over again. I call it "racial commentary." I call myself a Black queer storyteller, put that on my business cards. I pretend I am telling a different story each time I write a new essay or TV script. The same tale becomes a new testament when you scrub it clean of careless old white gods. But if cleanliness is next to godliness, isn't starting a new story without burning the old book just waiting for a resurrection? No wonder these gods keep coming back.

From time to time, I used to come to this steam room to cruise like the white man sitting across from me. I discovered that this little wooden box hidden behind the locker room was the temple my body was never allowed to be, and finding others who would finally pray with me a prayer I understood inside of it was liberating. I often tasted rebellion against the violent limits imposed around my Black queerness while cruising in the steam room. So I suppose it should come as no surprise that safety from his unwanted attention is not sanctioned when I've done so much behind a door with a sign reading, "INAPPROPRIATE

BEHAVIOR OF ANY KIND WILL NOT BE TOLERATED."
And I suppose you could also say that 500 years ago this world deemed my very existence inappropriate everywhere.

The steam room is the place where I met the last boy I dated without ever intending to love. He was Black, and he had been shooting me looks throughout my entire workout, and I would smile occasionally in return, just long enough to have plausible deniability if it came to it. Not-so-coincidentally, we finished and grabbed our towels at the same time. Never speaking a word, I opened the steam room door and walked into the plume of vapor knowing full well he would follow. Wanting him to. And perhaps what happened next is why I still expect this mist to carry me up toward someplace heavenly.

Behind the fog, the boy asked so many questions with his eyes that the white man wouldn't. *Is this okay? Do you want me to stop? Are you afraid?* I wanted to tell him with mine that I could not ever love him the way he would end up wanting me to, but even as a storyteller that was beyond the limits of what my eyes and words could say. Instead, I told him, "Yes. Don't stop. I am always afraid of sex. Let's be afraid together."

He would go on to court me for some time, persistent, but never too much. After coming to terms with the ultimate futility of us, he moved away, and I never heard from him again. That is the end of that story. That's how stories should end. But there are some books that simply refuse to close.

I have always been afraid of ghosts. I close my eyes in the steam room and hope that those who speak for my body somehow stay dead. But eventually I open my eyes again, I don't know why. And when I do, the white man in the steam room is masturbating.

==

My friend texted me today about how a group of white men at his gym similarly refused his rebuttals, how they kept coming onto him despite his death stares and despite him closing his eyes. We both have these experiences regularly at our apparently very queer frequented gyms, and have had this conversation together many times, so I knew what he was going to say before he said it. I also knew, because he's as light as me, someone, somewhere down the line of his family tree had already said it before the both of us. This might very well be anti-Black; I know Africans come in all shades. But I also know white men.

My friend didn't know how to make it stop, he says, so he left. I want to write that I leave too, after the white man sitting in front of me spreads his legs a little wider, erecting a tent with his penis and towel between his legs. When I write this story, I want to write it with flair. I want to write that this tent resembles hooded men and burning crosses, and invoke some profound message with that metaphor. I want to write it as though the steam is smoke, as though only a white god's burning crucifix can be the source of fire, as though I don't have the flame to set this world ablaze myself.

I want to write it and make *this* violence special because if I don't, who will? I want to write it and make *this* violence special because if it is not then what does it matter that I endured it? If my soul has already been stolen then what is left of me to be plundered? I don't know how to make it stop, I want to write, so I leave. At least a story you leave behind has an ending, even when it doesn't. At least then I won't have to admit how I looked at the man in the steam room for a moment, too. At least then I won't have to think about what that look meant. At least then I won't have to commit the violence I want to commit every time this happens, violence I know I won't get away with.

―

In another story, I watch the white man masturbate, or I hide behind the smoke, or I hold my breath until I pass out and never wake back up, but these are only different chapters to a book everyone wants but only to hard-read, still refusing to root for the characters. The alternative, burning this scripture, the story of Black queer people killing their tormentors rather than being killed by them, ends with the world putting such blasphemers in chains. So I leave the steam room triumphantly instead, my towel hanging down off my waist just slightly enough to feel the sigh he breathes onto the curve of my hip. I call this breath "disappointment," even as I hold the door behind me for another Black boy to enter as I walk out. I call this "leaving," but he always gets what he came for.

SAID THE POET

JENNY MOLBERG

You are a frozen pond with fish pulsing beneath Look in the mirror Say you're beautiful Why don't you touch me more Why are you holding yourself I killed the only pet I ever loved This isn't yelling This isn't my definition of yelling My own father yells until my mother is silent as a sea cave Asleep you are my bird underground in a box I want to touch all your feathers I swear I'll be better Wake up Your friends don't love you Your family doesn't love you I am a good person I am a good poet Once I stood on the train tracks too long I am the victim here I didn't sleep with that student Marry me I hated you last night Be the mother of my children I have a very good reputation My childhood was dappled with henbit Why won't you open the door Why aren't you answering me You should be ashamed of yourself You are a cricket I am the light Be with me forever Why are you afraid Get down on your knees and say you're sorry Have another drink Take off your clothes Try getting angry It feels so good

AT INTERNATIONAL JUDO CAMP

KYLE LOPEZ

Mandatory morning runs, a mile up Huguenot hills and back
before breakfast. Entering the dojo three times a day to train.
Sitting on the tatami in seiza, bowing, going through the motions.
Don't remember how many judokas I sparred with each night —
just lots of wins throwing a mean headlock, same as my dad,
his dad, and his. A boy taught me to say your mother sucks dicks
in Ukrainian, laughing as I learned each word. I remember knowing
on some level that wasn't what it meant, yet still parroting the words
for the other Ukrainian boys when prompted. The way they all
                                                    laughed.
Brittany crushed on me hard and wouldn't catch a hint,
not that I could either at fourteen. Don't remember being mean or
                                                    kind to her.
I remember a boy darting toward the lake with Alex's shoes,
Alex ballooning behind, too slow to halt their launch.
We watched those red and white blobs bob amidst the blue.
Another night, all the boys in my cabin filed into a room for some
                                                    speech.
All of us sardined in a standing pack, reek of Axe Body Spray in
                                                    the air,
the boy who threw Alex's shoes right behind me. He looked a head
taller, some span wider, couple years older. As the talk starts, his
                                                    hands grip
my shoulders how we grip the lapels on an opponent's gi.
A surprise vice. I remember not wanting to disrupt the speaker,
how handsome the boy's face was, how he covered my mouth
without touching it. His breath, angled downward—like
succulent chatter—as his hands lowered to the untouched,
unseen. No one knew. I remember my freeze, my confusion.

I'd only ever been pinned to the mat. This was like that.
No match, no score, just him.
Couldn't fathom it: how far from me I seemed, how hard
it all felt, how the room cleared out after he stopped
and we didn't speak again.

THE GIFT

RITA MARIA MARTINEZ

It's 1993 and it's Patty's birthday. She sits three seats in front of me
during our senior year of high school in Mr. H's religion class.

It's five minutes prior to the final bell most of us are seated.
A clique of boys has purchased a gift for the birthday girl

who is turning eighteen. One of the boys submits the white box.
In the movies, this box would contain flowers from a debonair

Cary Grant or Gary Cooper. Jenny would be a beaming Doris Day
opening her surprise, except it's 1993 and Patty's not an actress.

She slowly opens the narrow lid and parts the tissue paper
unearthing a vibrator. A collective gasp sweeps through the room

followed by a loud *Fuck You* as Jenny entombs the sex toy,
tells them to *use it on themselves*, and launches the box across

two rows until it hits one of the offenders with a loud thwack.
The pervs in the clique laugh like Biff from *Back to the Future*

when he sexually assaults Elaine in the car, his big paws *manoseando*,
a Spanish word that makes women cringe, slang that summons

images of "slutty chicks" being groped and discarded,
passed from one guy to the next like water in a bucket chain,

like the girl who is date-raped during spring break in *Where the Boys Are*,
except this isn't 1960 and this isn't a movie.

DATE GRAPE

FREESIA MCKEE

*"Brewer Responds to Protests
About Offensive Beer Name"*

—*MILWAUKEE JOURNAL SENTINEL*,
DECEMBER 7, 2016

What if I took the worst thing
that's happened to you
and joked about it

and joked about it
Using you as both
ammunition and target

Puckered up
shut down
What if I pit you

against yourself
Only a
joke Stoked to win

the same old contests
If I add some sour
to the sweetness

how does it taste?

Concord seedless
purple like a bruise
wrinkled fruit

The bitterest grape
the stapled shut lip
All the bars I've jumped

   over sleeping in anger
   holding
   that sour grape

   date rape

FOR A MINUTE THERE, I THOUGHT WE COULD'VE BEEN HAPPY

CATHLEEN CHAMBLESS

In a trailer park in a desert, Lassie met her first coyote. The coyote bowed down to her, his ears perked up and bushy tail wagging. She looked in his eyes and saw how they were silver with glimmers of honey. She couldn't help but curtsy and give him a playful bark as if to say *I dig you too, my dear.* He gave her a smile full of fangs so sexy. I dare you to follow me. He dashed off into the ravine and she sprung after him. She got to the bottom where he disappeared into a forest of prickly pear cacti, their fuchsia bulbs glowing like Chinese paper lanterns. The sunlight was so bright she could only see by squinting. Suddenly, she was slammed on her back, four coyotes ripping out her entrails and laughing, dragging her innards through the sand, snagging on the spines of the cactus branches. Coyotes only pretend to play like dogs when they're starving.

IV

HOME

TOO OLD FOR THAT, NOW

CARIDAD MORO

My father is a mercurial man, known for dark, brooding silences and piques of rage but also deep belly laughs, arresting charm, and an affectionate physicality with his children. Throughout my childhood he has jostled me on his shoulders, whinnied like a horse as I clung to his back, cradled me quietly on his lap in the flicker of prime-time television before carrying me to my room and tucking me in for the night.

I love him.

I live for those moments. In search of them, I have learned to gauge his mood, to read the electricity in the air around him, to discern when to approach, when to make myself scarce. I am very good at it.

One night I deem him mellow and amenable and I begin to scramble onto his lap in order to settle in and watch *The Waltons* when he pushes me away with the palms of his hands, raises his voice and says,

"Stop! You're too old for that, now."

I am eleven.

I want to ask why, but the air has been sucked out of my lungs as if I'd been punched in the gut, my throat obstructed by a fist of tears, so I say nothing. Frantically, I run through a laundry list of things I could have done to bring on this level of rejection: Had I uttered a smart remark? Forgotten to wash the dishes? Fought with my brother? Played, laughed, breathed too loud?

I can think of nothing I have done that would warrant the upending of such a tangible expression of his love.

I do not know what I've done, but I understand that the answer lies in the fact that he won't look at me after he says it, that he busies his hands with his lighter, his pack of Camel shorts, that he stares at the TV screen as I stare at the side of his face and wait for him to explain.

I know, too, that his reaction has something to do with the reason why some boys at school have begun to save seats for my friend Gina and me at their lunch tables, why they follow us to class and snap our newly acquired bras when the adults aren't looking, why those same boys, when choosing sides for volleyball, have begun to evaluate the girls using a new rubric they call the Cup and Jiggle Meter, which explains why Gina and I are suddenly first draft picks, even though I am not particularly athletic and have never, ever managed to see a set through to completion.

It is the same reason why the salesperson at the Lady's Intimates department on the second floor of Jordan Marsh whispers to my mother that perhaps I had skipped the training bra stage, handing me an A cup to try on while propelling me into a powder-pink dressing room where my mother watches me from a tufted chaise.

It dawns on me then, what I've done to deserve his rejection.

I like it.

I like the attention, like the way it feels to be seen, to be noticed, like the feel of my new breasts, like how my body looks in the mirror, like to cup them in the shower, like how they fill out the new peach and white bathing suit my mother let me buy on that trip to Jordan Marsh (in the Juniors section, a vast improvement from the ruffled assortment of suits in the Girls department), like how the suit, with its peephole halter top, holds my blooming flesh together, beautifully.

That I have dared to love my new curves this much makes me almost sick with shame, but it doesn't stop me from pulling on that very bathing suit two weeks later for a pool party at my best friend Arianna's house down the block. Our fathers play poker and dominoes together and our mothers exchange sewing patterns and recipes, so I am allowed to come and go to her house—the hub for all the kids on our block—with relative freedom, as long as my brother is with me.

When we get there, the pool is thick with kids and assorted adults who have been roped into endless games of Marco Polo and Chicken Fight matches. Ari sits perched on her father's shoulders and challenges me to a match. I am happy when her father's friend, known to me simply and affectionately as Papi, calls me over and offers to serve as my base. I swim over to him, ready to do battle.

I place my hands on his shoulders and prepare to lift myself onto his neck, but instead of squatting into the water so that I can propel myself up, he turns his body slightly and maneuvers his hand between my legs and strokes me—surely, deftly, purposely—under the guise of helping me up. I have never been touched in this way, but there is no mistaking the intention behind his caress. It is no accident, no poorly timed collision between us. No, his move is deliberate, and when I look up into his face his smile backs up what my body knows: he did this on purpose.

He liked it.

I kick my legs as hard as I can and propel my body away from his.

"Come on!" yells Ari. "What are you waiting for?"

I want to scream, tell everybody in that pool what he did, but instead I stay silent and begin to hate her for the danger she put me in from the safety of her father's arms. I duck under water so that the tears leaking from my eyes go unnoticed. I feign a cramp and practically run up the pool steps and out of the water.

I sit away from the rest of the party, shivering in the sun for so long that her mother approaches me and asks if I am alright. She is a kind woman, a woman who has fed me and cared for me during the many hours I have spent in her home, but I don't tell her what has happened. I don't think to warn her against a man who has easy proximity to her three daughters. I don't tell her because my boobs look big in my bathing suit and based on that I know she won't believe me.

Instead I tell her I don't feel well. She confirms I look very pale and offers to drive me the half a block it takes to get home. I decline her offer politely, grab my brother, and walk home. When we come through the door my father is doing yard work and my mother is cooking dinner. She calls from the kitchen, surprised we are back so soon, but neither of them sees me come in.

"It's Cary's fault," my brother says. "She feels sick," and I nod, because yes, yes, yes, it is my fault.

I take to my bed, blanketed in shame once again, but the shame has changed; it's weightier now, heavy with the knowing that I had brought on the violation with my breast-fueled glee, my whorish vanity, my desire to be seen. Surely, that's why he had chosen me, because somehow, he knew I deserved it.

I spend the rest of that afternoon in feverish starts and stops of sleep. I skip dinner and only emerge from my bedroom when my mother insists I join the rest of the family on the couch.

"*Love Boat* is on," she trills, oblivious.

When I approach the couch, my father looks at me for a beat too long and I'm sure he can see the defilement on me, yet something about the look on my face tugs on his heart for he does what he rarely does, reverses himself, holds out his arms and says,

"*Ven, mi niña*, come sit with your old man. You don't look so good."

The fist in my throat returns because I finally understand why he had pushed me away. I understand that he'd been trying to warn me away from the laps of men because the changes in my body made me bait for the taking, because laps and hands and the desires of men were dangerous—even if that lap was his.

The television screen doubles and triples in my vision when I finally respond to his request, my eyes forward, face turned away from him.

"No, Pop," I say, "I'm too old for that, now."

BLACKOUT

ELISA ALBO

New York, 1977

The pilot's voice quiets then concentrates the cabin—
New York, the entire city, is blacked out. We're landing
in Newark. I'm sixteen, flying alone for the first time.

On a bus to La Guardia I enter a city where someone
has pulled the plug—buildings, bridges, roads erased,
as if we've been struck blind. At the airport stranded

travelers sprawl on the floors of the airless terminal,
luggage and bodies strewn like stones in a black river
to trip the sightless, stumbling to find their way out

of the blackened building, into the blacker night. I hover
near the counter of my airline, decline the offers of taxi
and limo drivers looking shady in the lack of light.

Then like two welcome ghosts, my twenty-five-year-old
married cousins materialize before me. We drive down
eerie streets, headlights for semaphores, to the family

store. Like many shops, restaurants, and office buildings
in every borough, broken into, ransacked, looted. Where
earlier in the night, plainclothes policemen, guns drawn,

mistook my cousins for thieves. But I have been found.
I can wait for the lights. During my stay in their small
apartment, my cousin's husband comes to me in the early

morning hours and with his fingers breaks into my body.
Like a safecracker, spoiler, crook, he palms and plunders,
ignores people trapped in elevators or suffocating from

lack of air, slinks off like a thief. Fifteen years later, I walk
into a birthday party in Florida. This cousin is there. A light
flickers on, many lights, thousands, millions, as if someone

has turned on a city—its streetlamps, construction site night
lights, searchlights, Times Square, neon, fluorescent, bare
light bulbs dangling in interrogation rooms, the sun returning,

not gradually, in a flash, after an eclipse, its heat on the back
of the eyes so intense that all that was black—each crack and
crevice—is made visible, is made clear, and it burns like fury.

AT ANY AGE

ELISA ALBO

I'm nearly sixty in my mother's kitchen when she asks,
What happened at sixteen? How?

She's looking at me, her eyes a clear blue.

She knows I've written about it, gather the stories
of others, turn trauma into art. I tell her,

>   With his fingers.
>   He put them inside. *Hijo puta*, she says.
>   I lay on a sofa, didn't move, didn't speak.

My cousin—her beloved niece married less than a year—
lay sleeping on the other side of the wall in
their tiny apartment in Bayside, New York.

>   He whispered, *Meet me in the shower.*
>   I dug into the sofa seam, blanket over my head,
>   frozen, until the front door clicked shut.

Why didn't you tell me?
I did, several times, tried to.
You didn't, couldn't, hear it,
got annoyed when I showed him
contempt, skipped family gatherings.

I thought it was my fault.

Took me years to realize, get angry.

She gazes at me. Even with her sight failing,
she can see. And she's pissed.

My mother is seventy-seven, fragile health.
Each person who connected him to us—her sister,
her nieces—has died. I step through this door.

I think he molested his daughter, will never
forget how she cried out, *Don't touch me!
Get away from me!*

when we walked into her bedroom
one night to check on her.

You were there. She was three years old.

I pray for his daughter from his second marriage.

The next year, my younger sister went to New York,
stayed with these cousins. He did it to her, too,
we learned, years later, when wounds found
words, too late for warnings.

A ROOT

ANNIE FINCH

What happened when he grabbed me at the root?
I stopped. It all stopped: spirals fought to win
My spiral life (from an unspiraled root) —

From thick cigar stubbed in my young tongue's root —
(Heart beating uncle lifetimes through my skin).
What happened, when he grabbed me at the root

Where women come to starve, our ready root?
My broken body (one more), broken in?
My spiral life from an unspiraled root-

Fed pomegranate? (in the basement: root-
Husked hell of seed as if seed could have been
What happened.) When he grabbed me at the root,

Did ancestors throw chains down through our root
To rot and winnow, with their pain and sin,
My spiral life? From an unspiraled root?

Oh sisters, keen our sisters! Till the root
Of loving! burns! (but not! from! foreign kin!)
WHAT happened (when) (he) (grabbed) me at the root?
Our spiral life! From an unspiraled root!

THE THINGS MA SAYS

BOSCH JONES

My blood pressure is rising.

Give me a kiss goodbye.

I swear to God, you touchhole.

You make this shit up I swear.

It doesn't matter how big your hard-on is

if you give me diamonds then I know you
love me.

Stop trying to shove it in when it's soft.

This is a fucking joke.

You were never fat.

You never had that before, you touch.

THE LION HEAD BELT BUCKLE

VIRGIL SUAREZ

My father bought it for me as a gift in the Madrid *rastro*
near where we lived, new immigrants from Cuba.

The eyes and mane carved deep into the metal, the tip of the nose
already thin with the blush of wear. My mother found a brown

leather strap and made it into a belt with enough slack and holes
to see me wearing it in Los Angeles where we landed next.

My father worked at Los Dos Toros, a meat market run by Papito,
A heavy-set man with a quick smile, and when I would visit

the market after school to wait for my father to bring me home,
Papito always talked to me about baseball and his favorite

Cincinnati Reds players. It was there one of his employees,
a skinny man with deep set eyes and crow-feather black

hair, would stop me in the narrow hallway by the produce tables
and grab the belt buckle and praise it. All along passing his hand

over my penis. "You are strong," he would whisper, "like this lion."
I would recoil from his touch and move away back to the front

where Papito would ask me about what bases I intended
to play next season on Los Cubanitos team. I never told my father,

or anyone, but the afternoon I showed up and the Fire Department
and police and ambulances huddled in the alleyway behind

Los Dos Toros, I knew something terrible had happened. Some
other kid had uttered the man's groping and insisting on a kiss

in the *almacén*, the darkened storage room past the meat locker.
And another father had taken matters into his own hands.

But instead I found my father hosing the back door entrance,
washing the blood down to the alleyway. He told me to wait for him

in the car. The paramedics rolled out Papito, shot and dead on a
    stretcher,
victim of a hold-up. The dark Cuban man who'd felt me up time

and again stood in the shade of a tree weeping and kicking the dirt
with blood encrusted shoes. I found out later he was the one who

slammed the assailant against the wall, and beat him unconscious.
Fuerte como un leon. The words fluttered like cow birds in the back

of my mind. Scattershot and ringing like the violence among the men.

X MARKS THE SPOT

OLIVER BRANTOME

i'd like to think you know what you did.
that you have a moral compass that tells you
putting yourself that far south on a three year old girl
is not the way to find your treasure.
you stole gems from me, jewels
that could've amounted to something
as i grew.
you ripped and pried gold chips from my hands,
small and frail.
i am not a treasure box.
you cannot dig deep inside me and find riches —
but you tried anyway.

THOSE SUNDAYS

CHRISTOPHER SOTO

My father worked too many hours. He'd come home with his
cracked hands and bad attitude. & I'd rather talk about Rory now.
[His blond locks] How the sun would comb crowns into his hair.
Rory was my first love, before he killed himself.

My father hated faggots. The way my cock looked beneath a
dress. The mismatch of his chafed knuckles and my cut cuticles.
A scrambling of hands. I was always running. Mascara.
Massacre.
My momma would wash the red paint off my nails and face.
She'd hold me like the frame of a house. No, the bars of a prison
cell.

"Mijo, your father is coming home soon. Hide your heels." I'm
the donkey clanking down the hall. Click, Clack, Click, Clack.
Over Momma's body [he'd grab me] & throw me against the
wall. My bruises dark as holes, he punched into the wall. His
hand was the hammer. I was the nail. & I want to talk about Rory
now.

That night, after my father smashed the television glass with his
baseball bat, I met Rory at the park. We made a pipe out of a
plastic bottle and aluminum foil. [He watched me undress & run
through ticking sprinklers.] I fell beside him then; beneath the
maple tree. & he saw my goose bumps from the cold. & he felt
my bruises, as they became a part of him.

Rory, I want to say that death is what you've always wanted. But that can't be the Truth. [This time] we can blame it on me. I'll be the packing mule, carry all the burden. & you, you can be a child again; fold your church hands like dirty laundry [crease them

tight].

Nobody has to know about us, not my father nor yours—
No, not even God.

LEARNING

GAIL CARSON LEVINE

Allie rolls her jeans halfway up her calves,
nothing to catch the gears.
She carries her helmet
over her forearm like a purse.
Using her allowance money,

she rents a bike and wheels it east.
At River Bridge Park, she sees
only one person she knows,
Stan's father, Mr. Bernstein, on a bench
watching his toddler daughter

in the sandbox. They say "Hi."
Allie walks the bike to the balustrade
and puts on the helmet, Mr. Bernstein
her goal; she will know how to ride
by the time she reaches him. She mounts,

fails to pedal but doesn't fall,
tries again, advancing in failure.
She almost completes a spin
when he walks to her.
"You'll never learn like that. I'll hold it

to get you started." He swears
not to tell Stan she didn't know how to ride.
Allie places her foot, begins to rise.
Mr. Bernstein grabs her ass, his fingers probing.
Ahead, his daughter plunges a red shovel into the sand.

TELLING

IVONNE LAMAZARES

This really happened:

My father said, "Come here."

He said, "Stop watching filthy *telenovelas*. You should be reading books."

"Sit here," he motioned. "Come sit."

I didn't know him well. We'd last seen each other in Cuba when I was six. Now I was fifteen. His mother and I had just arrived in Miami and I was getting to know him again.

He pointed to his lap. I sat between his knees.

"Look here," he said. His breath was acrid. He'd been drinking. I didn't know many things, but I could figure out the vinegar smell of drinking. He said, "You need to be smart. Time will tell if you're smart."

It was late. The parking lot of the Sevilla Gardens Apartments in Hialeah was quiet except for the occasional car clearing the speed bumps. Abuela was snoring in the bedroom. I had my nightgown on. I was going to bed. "You and I know what's what," he said. "We know. It's between us." He looked at me as if he were about to quiz me on a math problem, then kissed me on the lips. My eyes stayed open. His tongue bumped against my front teeth. "Other people don't understand." He held my hand. His palm was rough. "What do you want to be when you grow up?"

"I want to be a writer," I said. I didn't know if I wanted to or not. It was a thought I had sometimes. I looked to see if this pleased him. I wanted to get up, too, and turn on all the lights.

"A writer. Well." He let out a breath. His other hand went distractedly up my thigh. "To be a writer you must have something to say." His hand lingered. "Time will tell."

PSYCH WARD

COLLEEN SUTTON

The fluorescent lights are bright. It's daytime outside and the sun is shining, but you wouldn't know it in here. The paint is missing in parts, the room is bare. There are two chairs, in pukey pastel pink. One has the stuffing pulled out.

In tandem, my husband is brought to another room. They won't let him stay with me. His room has the same pukey pink chairs, but they're intact, and there's a nice flatscreen in the corner. The news is playing silently, closed captioning below it. The nurse tells him to feel free to change the channel. Would he like some water? A coffee? He's worried about me, but he feels confident and in control of himself. He's there to help, not to get help.

I sit alone and wait, staring at the two chairs. They're so ugly. Who chose such ugly chairs? I see a bite mark and realize the stuffing has been ripped out by teeth. I look more closely. The paint's not peeling; someone has ripped nails down the walls, tearing paint in chunks along the way. I look up at the fluorescent light and see it's covered with a sweet little steel cage. The desk is bolted to the floor. The chairs are bolted to the floor. The feeling in my belly intensifies. What if they keep me here? What if this is where I belong?

The nurse had left the door open. I can see into the corridor—workers walking this way and that. Then I see two police officers, escorting a man. He's not old, maybe 20-something. He's agitated. "Hi, Michael," a nurse gently calls out to him as he walks by. I hear bits and pieces of what he's saying to the officers. "It's just, it's just my dad makes me so mad sometimes. I just get so mad . . . but I'm ok now" his voice trails off as he turns the corner.

Two nurses walk by. ". . . Michael's back . . . ," one sighs.

I look back at the chair with the bite marks; I look at the

wall, the ripped paint, the dirty fingerprints. How long would it take before I'd start taking chunks out of the chair? I purse my lips, that color, a hospital . . . I'm hesitant to even touch it with my butt while I'm sitting down. Looks like I've got a while before I start biting shit.

The Doctor finally comes in. He asks me why I'm here. I tell him I just need a prescription and then I can go. I tell him I'm good, I'm ok. I promise.

The more I repeat it, the less convinced he is. He asks what I'm anxious about. I tell him the story that's become rote now: the assault in a faraway country; the loss of my job afterwards; the various diagnoses from so many doctors until they settled on PTSD. He focuses on the assault. They always focus on the assault. There was the violation of the man's hands in my underwear; his fingers with the clean nailbeds; the gun against my temple. Worse is the violation of repeating this story to each new man. Justifying myself. Male police; male doctors; my male bosses. Eight months later, I still feel like a fraud. No rape just . . . other stuff. Only my shorts were torn. I was intact. And yet here I am, C. Sutton, BA, MSc, PTSD.

I start to cry, I lose air. I read it on his face. He doesn't believe me. I start repeating myself, throwing the words at him, one after another. ". . . the man held the gun throughout . . . and then he . . . but that wasn't the worst . . ." I bend over and throw up. Right there on the laminate hospital floor. They should have bolted down a wastepaper basket too.

The Doctor hands me Kleenex, a metal tray. Is this a bedpan? I don't care; I throw up in that. Once the heaving stops, he leaves me again. I try to get myself together. I know this game. I have to be composed or they won't let me leave. But the more I think of it, the less air I can get inside.

The door opens. It's my husband. He's the best thing I've ever seen. I tell him I'm scared. He reassures me: they chatted with him, asked him some questions, no big deal. Once he confirmed the same story, the assault, my boss, they were relieved; they'd renew my prescription, no problem. I won't have to stay in the hospital. And just like that, there's air again.

When the Doctor comes in a final time, he's so kind. He tells me I'm strong. He believes me. Suddenly I'm myself again. I'm not that other girl, that girl gasping for air, tears running while she threw up in a bedpan. He escorts us to the exit doors, but they're electronically bolted shut.

"Oops, here, let me get that for you." The Doctor reaches forward with his pass.

"Why are they bolted?" I ask.

"Not everyone's like you, Colleen."

I look at my husband. I think of how much his story today mattered. How much his presence mattered. I think about my family at home, ready to drop everything and come get me.

I think about Michael. Where's his father? Why is he all alone in this terrifying place? In the room with the bitten chairs bolted to the floor, the nail marks down the walls like something out of a horror film. If I had come in alone, would I have been treated like Michael? Would they have believed me?

We walk out into the sunshine. My husband looks at me, puts his arm around me. "You're not like them," he says. "You're not anything like Michael or those people that have to be locked in." I nod my head. I want to believe that, but I'm not so sure. Give me the wrong circumstances, and I'll give you Michael.

BECAUSE WHAT WE DO DOES NOT DIE

ELLEN BASS

This is not his voice. This is not his tongue.
This is a praise song
for the mother who sat down beside me,
her coat still on, saying,
What is it, Ellen? This is praise
to the wasp mother
who hissed, *The bastard. The son of a bitch,*
who repeated it over and over,
I'm sorry you didn't bite his tongue off.
Poke his eyes out.
And the next day told him,
You have guts to come back here.
If you ever touch Ellen again, I'll tell your wife.
If you see her on the street, cross
and walk on the other side.
The man protested. *I didn't do anything.*
He needed the job. *I only kissed her.*
He had a five-year-old daughter. My mother asked,
How would you like it if Mr. Bass kissed
your daughter that way?
The man blanched. My mother fired him.
I never saw him again. Maybe that's why
I can't picture him now. My mother erased him.
This is how I bow down to my mother,
my dead mother who will never be dead,
because what we do does not die, does not splinter
or stutter away. She could never have known

how her fury would fatten me
to write the thousands of sentences
in *The Courage to Heal*. This is how
I put on my flowered dress and flew
across the continent, walked onto any stage
and stood there while the tech slid the cord
of the mic down my spine, how I sat
next to any man—or any woman—who tried
to deny or defuse or desecrate the truth.
I could—and did—walk to my chair
and lay my bare arm on the armrest first,
claiming the space. And even when
those talk show hosts, even Oprah herself—
this was that long ago when she was still silent—
did nothing, nothing at all, to defend
the survivors or defend me, I knew
there was a woman somewhere sitting on her couch
still in her bathrobe. And this is when
I looked directly into the camera.
This is when I spoke.

GENDER BENDER

JENNIFER MICHAEL HECHT

Evolution settles for a while on various stable balances.
One is that some of the girls like cute boys and some
like ugly older men and sometimes women. The difference
between them is the ones who like older men were felt up

by their fathers or uncles or older brothers, or if he didn't
touch you, still you lived in his cauldron of curses and
urges which could be just as worse. They grow already old,
angry and wise, they get rich, get mean, get theirs.

The untouched-uncursed others are happy never needing
to do much, and never do much more than good. They envy
their mean, rich, talented, drunk sisters. Good girls drink milk
and make milk and know they've missed out and know they're

better off. They might dance and design but won't rip out lungs
for a flag. Bad ones write books and slash red paint on canvas;
they've rage to vent, they've fault lines and will rip a toga off
a Caesar and stab a goat for the ether. It's as simple as that.

Either, deep in the dark of your history, someone showed you
that you could be used as a cash machine, as a popcorn popper,
as a rocket launch, as a coin-slot jackpot spunker, or they didn't
and you grew up unused and clueless. Either you got a clue

and spiked lunch or you got zilch but no punch. And you
never knew. It's not exactly anyone's fault. If it happened
and you don't like older men that's just because you like
them so much you won't let yourself have one. If you did

everyone would see. Then they would know what happened
a long time ago, with you and with that original him, whose eyes
you've been avoiding for decades gone forgotten. That's why
you date men smaller than you or not at all. Or maybe you've

turned into a man. It isn't anyone's fault; it is just human
and it is what happens. Or doesn't happen. That's that. Any
questions? If you see a girl dressed to say, "No one tells me
what to do," you know someone once told her what to do.

IN MEMORIAM, ANN

DEBRA DEAN

Here by way of a Louisiana parish, our wonder woman was too well-bred to curse or push like a New Yorker. Shy and porcelain pale, she gave the impression of floating into a room like a soap bubble, iridescent, beautiful and delicate. But if you looked more closely, her wispy arms were reeds of muscle. Her quiet smile was resolve.

At twenty-seven, she'd already had a kidney transplant. Years later, long after she left the city, she would battle leukemia and then breast cancer. She was fierce then, too, but this is the story we all like to tell.

She's taking the rush hour subway home. Doors open, more people squeeze in, and they're packed together, hanging from straps, grasping poles, sharing the steamy air.

She feels the impression of a hand. Not glancing. Insinuating. Fingers.

Like a flash, she grabs a thick wrist and thrusts it upwards in the air.

"Is *this* the hand?" she shouts. "Is *this* the hand that grabbed my ass?"

She holds him captive in her grip so that everyone in the car can get a good, long look. Pins him like a moth to the Truth.

Then she lets him go. The others glare and heckle as he slinks through the car, threaten to take him apart, the creepy shit. They roil and shove, until he escapes through the end door into the next car.

As the fury ebbs from her blood, she answers politely that she is fine, thank you very much. Yes. Truly. Fine.

Slowly, the placid waters of the bayou close over the dark thing, swallow it whole.

And she is still there, floating still.

BLINDSIDED

ANGELA BONAVOGLIA

The house where Mr. M. and his family live is one block up from ours. It's big. They have a brand-new car. They live, says my mother, "on easy street." But they are churchgoing people, active in our Catholic parish, embraced by our spiritual community.

It's a summer day, and I'm nine years old. I set out to visit their daughter, Claire. I'm happy to be walking in the sunshine to see my friend. I like her very much. I like her little sister Amy, and her older brother Jeff, too. Her mother I don't like so much. She's stiff, unfriendly. She always seems to be mad. I definitely don't like Claire's father. He's always yelling at his wife, and he's mean to his son. One day, as I'm passing by, I see Jeff come flying out of their yard onto the sidewalk, pushed by his red-faced, raging father, who is calling him a "lug" and a "son of a bitch." I'm sure other people saw similar incidents, but no one took action in those days—it was nobody's business.

On this particular day, I turn into their yard, and head up the long, steep flight of stairs to the small, enclosed back porch. I knock. Mr. M. appears inside the screen door. He's very tall. I've never encountered him alone.

"Hi," I say, tentatively, craning my neck to look up at him. "Is Claire home?"

He looks down at me. He opens the door. I expect him to speak. Instead, he sweeps me off my feet. Suddenly, he shoves his hand under my dress, past my panties, and swift as a rattler's fangs, plunges his bony fingers into my vagina.

I'm a rag doll now, suspended in mid-air. Time stops. He lets out a smug, throaty laugh, carries me into the kitchen, and lowers me down the long, long way to the floor. He heads for the living room. I stand alone, bewildered, stunned, and conscious

189

of a secret part of me in a way I'd never been before, as if it's no longer mine, is public somehow, exposed.

I don't know what happened after that. Where he went. Where I went.

Days, months, years go by. I have no words to describe what Mr. M. did to me, so I tell no one, not even my beloved mother, until decades later, after she tells me what happened to her as a child, at the hands of her own father.

But I have seen at an early age the harm that men can do to women, how hard it can be to fight back, and that sometimes, maybe most times, you don't even see it coming.

FIRST KISS

LYNNE BARRETT

At fifteen, I was a popular babysitter, good with kids and bookish, not the type to sneak a boyfriend in.

On this spring night when the parents got home, past ten, a little late, I was ready to go, children asleep, homework in my book bag. Mrs. M (not her real initial) rustled past me to get money from the bedroom. Mr. M, by the door, jingled keys. I'd walked here, but dads were expected to drive younger babysitters home after dark, despite everyone knowing everyone in our safe neighborhood.

I could tell they'd been drinking. My father drank beer, sometimes shots of rye. My mother turned pink after one cocktail.

Mr. M gave an impression of money and solidity—broad jaw, bulky shoulders. Dad called him a stuffed shirt. My mother admired Mrs. M's style. She'd often mention when they'd had coffee or volunteered together.

I slipped the cash into my jeans as the front door clicked shut behind us. I was wearing a short-sleeved top, I remember, the night warm. Mr. M's car was parked on the street, aimed towards my house.

He held the passenger door open for me. Cars still had wide sofa front seats then. I fastened my seat belt. Through the open windows, I smelled lilacs. He walked around, got in, and started the car.

I expected him to put on headlights, to shift, but he leaned over, braced one hand by my right shoulder, and kissed me wetly on the mouth.

I stayed still, lips pressed closed, holding my breath, till he pulled back, put on the headlights, and drove.

I kept my mouth shut. What was wrong with him? To do

that? Right outside their house? Was he very drunk? Some fathers tried to chat, but none touched me. I felt sad for his children, his wife. But mostly I wondered how I'd tell my mother. She had such belief in other people's normalcy. She wouldn't want my dad to know: my dad would kill him. But wouldn't she feel she had to tell Mrs. M? And if not, still, she'd carry the knowledge. Either way, I would destroy the friendship.

I thought of ways to avoid working there anymore. And soon I'd be sixteen, old enough to walk home alone. By the time I could see the lit lamp by our front steps, I'd accepted the burden of silence.

SEVEN TIMES SEVEN

TRISH MACENULTY

When he grabbed my mother around the neck,
dragged her through the kitchen,
through the busted back door,
I was seven. Never saw him before
or since but he stayed,
an unwanted visitor in my psyche.

Nothing got rid of him. Not the drugs,
not the drink, not the men,
whose hearts I grabbed, twisted
in angry fists.

Have we come to peace,
the man who took my mother
to ground, whispered against
her neck with a knife as sirens
made a doleful sound, and I,
no longer seven? Jesus said,
forgive seven times seven.

I suppose that's how many times
it takes to forgive what you
can never forget.

AFTERWORD

Anita Hill

In 1978, during my second year of law school, I rediscovered poetry. My friend Greg gave me a copy of Ntozake Shange's book *For Colored Girls Who Have Considered Suicide When the Rainbow Is Enuf.* Like most high school students in the '70s, I had been taught the American poets, most of them white males. In my farewell class speech, I quoted Robert Frost, "miles to go before I sleep," as a nod to my teachings and a polite way of showing my eagerness to move on to the next phase of my life.

After four years of an undergraduate curriculum loaded with science courses and a year of law classes preparing me to "think like a lawyer," I needed to return to poetry. More specifically, I needed Shange's poetry—to hear the "words of a young black girl's growing up, her triumphs & errors, our struggle to become all that is forbidden by our environment, all that is forfeited by our gender, all that we have forgotten."

And my reunion could not have happened at a better time. Law school was one of the most alienating experiences of my life. *For Colored Girls* spoke to the questions that I and my African American women classmates had about life, struggles, pain, and joy. The words also resonated with the six thousand people a week who experienced the choreopoem's production at the Booth Theatre. Ms. Shange reminded all of us that we were not disembodied minds, and that our bodies were both gendered and raced in ways over which we had little control. And that the reality of our experiences mattered in how we understood the law and influenced the value the law assigned to us. Reading Shange and then seeing a performance of *For Colored Girls* allowed me to return to the law and in my own voice "sing the song of [my] possibilities."

Over the years, I learned the importance of taking that reality into account in my law practice and my teaching. My respect for the law and what has been accomplished through it continued. But my faith in the law as a means for positive change only continued because I know it can evolve to do better. In 1982 Professor Robert Cover's admonition that "no set of legal institutions or prescriptions exists apart from the narratives that locate it and give it meaning" gave me a new sense of the law's potential. Having moved from a corporate law firm to working in a civil rights office in the federal Department of Education, I set about hearing the narratives that would give meaning to the law's promise of equal educational opportunity.

I soon realized that addressing gendered and racialized violence and indifference was necessary in order for any portion of the promise of equality to be fulfilled. I recalled the words of Ntozake Shange and other authors. I revisited the works of Zora Neale Hurston and Toni Morrison and turned to Alice Walker, Isabel Allende, and Amy Tan. In the 1970s and '80s, these were the writers who, for me, acknowledged the unique normative worlds we occupy that govern our lives, but often ignore our assorted realities.

In time, I, along with others, broadened our understanding of the narratives that give law its meaning. No longer wedded to case-law storytelling as the sole source of defining civil rights law's purpose, we drew upon poetry and prose to learn how to make sure that law became more than "a system of rules to be observed, but [instead becomes] a world" serving different human beings with diverse experiences and needs striving for equality.

Under the Civil Rights Act of 1964, sexual harassment is defined as persistent or severe, unwelcome or unwanted, sexual behavior. Today, based on the protections developed over four decades of case law, behavior ranging from verbal sexual slurs and abuses to sexual extortion and rape are deemed violations of an individual's civil rights. Prohibited behavior includes demands for sex in exchange for employment, pay raises, job retention, or promotions. And hostile sexual behavior that taints the work environment making it difficult or impossible to function is forbidden under Title VII as well. Sexual harassment cases from the '70s through the first eighteen years of the twenty-first century describe conduct inexplicable in its shocking brutality: like the bank manager who forced an employee to have sex with him as many as fifty times over the course of a three-year employment or the employee who began to get poor performance reviews after she complained about supervisors who questioned her about her "sexual proclivities" and suggested she go with them to motels.

Yet, no matter how similar to others' experiences, the facts as written in cases always fail to capture the full impact of being "grabbed" verbally or physically. Case reports can gloss over the anguish and trauma sexual violations generate in the name of legal dogma. And sadly, legal opinions do little to create the community needed to show survivors and victims that they are not alone and to show the rest of us that the suffering of sexual violations is a matter of public concern.

It would take a survey conducted in 1976 by *Redbook* magazine to make the public aware of the "age-old problem" of sexual harassment, a problem that the popular publication declared to be shrouded in silence but that was suddenly "out of the closet." Well before the internet and telephones made polling convenient, some nine thousand women responded to a mail-in questionnaire that found that nine out of ten respondents said they had been subjected to unwanted sexual advances at work. The survey participants described in their own terms what they had endured and how they and others had reacted. The responses might have been shocking but for the fact that they described experiences that were so common for so many women.

Why a *Redbook* poll? Because, notwithstanding the number of important cases that were filed during the period, little public attention was being paid to the problem. Through cases, the legal system was put on notice of the horrific threats that women were confronting, in the workplace and in classrooms and on campuses and at home and on the streets. But in the '70s, the federal justice system did very little to discover the prevalence of sexual violations in the workplace, and data on other violent victimization, particularly of women, was lacking.

Even today, not enough is being done to understand the social or political ecologies in which bullying, harassment, grabbing, groping, assault, and rape flourish and yet go unaddressed. In *For Colored Girls*, Ntozake Shange's chorus of women who lament being "betrayed by men who know us" reflects the prevalence of acquaintance violations. Without a video, "date" and "spousal" rape, incest, and other family abuse claims are difficult to prosecute in criminal proceedings and rarely find their way to civil courts. But Morrison's *The Bluest Eye* can shine a bright light on the misogyny and racism that allows them to happen.

The law needs poetry, just as it needs essays and novels that explain how mouths, hands, telephones, cars, playgrounds, family and neighborhood gatherings, and workplaces are weaponized to undermine the bodily integrity of the less powerful. The law needs prose and poems that expose the anguish and trauma survivors suffer even after the slurs and verbal affronts have left the mouths of our abusers and the fingermarks, welts, and bruises are no longer visible.

We need the means to bring the songs of survivors and those who would be survivors to each other and to bystanders in ways that elevate the experiences to social and legal consciousness. We need *Grabbed* to bring humanity into our public conversation and into the law that mediates sexual and gendered violence and opens our understanding to the many factors, like race, sexual and gender identity, class, and religion, to name just a few, that enable and excuse them both.

EDITORS

ELISA ALBO is the author of *Passage to America*, poems that recount her family immigrant story, and *Each Day More*, a collection of elegies. Her poems have appeared in journals such as *Alimentum, Bomb, Crab Orchard Review, InterLitQ, MiPoesias, Notre Dame Review, Poetry East, SWWIM*, and *Zing Magazine*, and in such anthologies as *Irrepressible Appetites, The Shelter of Politics, Tigertail: A South Florida Annual, Two Countries: Daughters and Sons of Immigrant Parents*, and *Vinegar and Char*. She has an MFA from Florida International University and teaches English and ESL at Broward College. She lives with her husband and daughters in Ft. Lauderdale, Florida.

RICHARD BLANCO is an American poet, public speaker, author, and civil engineer. Having read for Barack Obama's second inauguration, he is the first immigrant, first Latino, first openly gay person, and the youngest person to be the US inaugural poet. Blanco's books of poetry include *City of a Hundred Fires, Directions to the Beach of the Dead*, and *How to Love a Country*. He was named a Woodrow Wilson Visiting Fellow and has received honorary doctorates from Macalester College, Colby College, and the University of Rhode Island. He has been featured on *CBS Sunday Morning*, NPR's *All Things Considered* and *Fresh Air* with Terry Gross, as well as major media from around the world. Blanco's poems and essays have appeared in numerous publications and anthologies, including the Best American Poetry series, the *New Yorker, The Nation*, the *New Republic, Huffington Post*, and *Condé Nast Traveler*.

CARIDAD MORO is the award-winning author of *Visionware*, published by Finishing Line Press as part of its New Women's Voices Series. She is the recipient of an Elizabeth George Foundation Grant and a Florida Individual Artist Fellowship in poetry. Her poems and essays have been nominated for the Pushcart Prize and

Best of the Net and have appeared in numerous publications and anthologies, including the Best American Poetry series, *Rhino*, *Reading Queer: Poetry in a Time of Chaos*, *Pintura/Palabra Project*, *Bridges To/From Cuba*, and the *Antioch Review*. She is the associate editor for the daily online literary journal *SWWIM Every Day*. Moro is also an English professor at Miami Dade College and Florida International University. She resides in Miami, Florida, with her wife and son.

NIKKI MOUSTAKI, author of the memoir *The Bird Market of Paris*, holds an MA in poetry from New York University, an MFA in poetry from Indiana University, and an MFA in fiction from New York University. She has taught creative writing at both of those universities, as well as at the New School in New York City and Miami Dade College in Florida. She is the recipient of a National Endowment for the Arts grant in poetry, along with many other national writing awards. Her poetry, fiction, and essays have appeared in various newspapers and literary magazines, anthologies, and college textbooks, including the *New York Times*, *Good Housekeeping*, *Publishers Weekly*, the *Village Voice*, and the *Miami Herald*, and her work has been featured in *Glamour*, *O, the Oprah Magazine*, and *Elle*, and on NPR. She is the author of *The Complete Idiot's Guide to Writing Poetry* and the poetry collection *Extremely Lightweight Guns*.

FOREWORD CONTRIBUTOR

JOYCE MAYNARD is the author of nine novels and three memoirs, including the *New York Times* best-selling novels *To Die For* and *Labor Day* (both adapted for film) and the best-selling memoir *At Home in the World*, which has been translated into sixteen languages. Her most recent memoir, *The Best of Us*—about finding her husband and losing him to cancer four years later—was published in 2017. Her new novel—her tenth—will be published in 2020. In 2002, Maynard founded the Lake Atitlan Writing Workshop in San Marcos La Laguna, Guatemala, where she hosts a weeklong workshop in personal storytelling every winter, as well as a summer memoir workshop in her home state of New Hampshire. She is a fellow of the MacDowell Colony and Yaddo.

AFTERWORD CONTRIBUTOR

ANITA HILL is a University Professor of Law, Public Policy, and Women's Studies in the Heller Graduate School of Policy and Management at Brandeis University in Waltham, Massachusetts, and the chair of the Commission to Eliminate Sexual Harassment and Advance Equality in the Workplace. Hill is the youngest of thirteen children from a farm in Oklahoma. She received her JD from Yale Law School in 1980. She began her career in private practice in Washington, DC. There she also worked at the US Department of Education and the Equal Employment Opportunity Commission. In 1989 Hill became the first African American to be tenured at the University of Oklahoma, College of Law, where she taught contracts and commercial law.

In December of 2017, Professor Hill became the chair of the Hollywood entertainment industry's Commission to Eliminate Sexual Harassment and Advance Equality in the Workplace. In that role she works to establish a best-practices and policies framework for addressing workplace abuses and discrimination and creating more equitable work environments throughout the industry.

Professor Hill's books include *Speaking Truth to Power* and *Reimagining Equality: Stories of Gender, Race, and Finding Home* (Beacon Press, 2011), the latter an analysis of the housing-market collapse of 2008 and its impact on gender and racial equality. Professor Hill is also currently engaging prominent academics and business professionals all over the country to spearhead the Gender/Race Imperative, a project to revive awareness of the broad capacity of Title IX, the crucial law mandating equal education opportunities for women. The Gender/Race Imperative will kickstart inquiry as well as legal and policy reforms that empower girls and women of all races and economic backgrounds for success in schools and workplaces.

LYNNE BARRETT is the recipient of the Florida Book Awards gold medal for fiction and the Edgar Award for best mystery story. Barrett teaches in the MFA program at Florida International University and is the editor of the *Florida Book Review*.

ELLEN BASS's poetry books include *Like a Beggar*, *The Human Line*, and *Mules of Love*. She coedited the first major anthology of women's poetry, *No More Masks!* Among her awards are fellowships from the National Endowment for the Arts and the California Arts Council, three Pushcart Prizes, the Lambda Literary Award, the Pablo Neruda Prize, the Larry Levis Prize, and the New Letters Prize. A chancellor of the Academy of American Poets, she teaches in the MFA writing program at Pacific University.

RUTH BEHAR is the Victor Haim Perera Collegiate Professor of Anthropology at the University of Michigan, a MacArthur Fellow, the recipient of a Guggenheim Fellowship, and was recently recognized as a "Great Immigrant" by the Carnegie Corporation. Her books include *Translated Woman: Crossing the Border with Esperanza's Story*, *The Vulnerable Observer: Anthropology That Breaks Your Heart*, *An Island Called Home: Returning to Jewish Cuba*, and *Traveling Heavy: A Memoir in between Journeys*.

ANGELA BONAVOGLIA is an author, a journalist, and a blogger who is nationally recognized for her writing about the contemporary crisis in the Catholic Church, including her most recent book, *Good Catholic Girls: How Women Are Leading the Fight to Change the Church*.

LAURE-ANNE BOSSELAAR is the author of *The Hour Between Dog and Wolf*, *Small Gods of Grief*, which won the Isabella Gardner Prize for Poetry in 2001, and of *A New Hunger*, an ALA Notable Book. Her latest collection, *These Many Rooms*, is out from Four Way Books. A Pushcart Prize recipient and the editor of four anthologies, she teaches at the Low-Residency MFA in Creative Writing Program of Pine Manor College, in Boston.

OLIVER BRANTOME is an English and art history student at Florida International University. Their work has been published in *Apogee Literary Journal* and *Into the Void* magazine. They reside in Miami, Florida.

JERICHO BROWN is the recipient of the 2020 Pulitzer Prize for Poetry for his book *The Tradition*, a Whiting Award, and fellowships from the John Simon Guggenheim Foundation, the Radcliffe Institute for Advanced Study at Harvard University, and the National Endowment for the Arts. He is an associate professor and the director of the Creative Writing Program at Emory University.

MARCI CALABRETTA CANCIO-BELLO is the author of *Hour of the Ox*, which won the 2015 AWP Donald Hall Prize for Poetry and the 2016 Florida Book Awards bronze medal for poetry. She has received poetry fellowships from Kundiman, the Knight Foundation, and the American Literary Translators Association.

NICOLE CALLIHAN's poetry books include *SuperLoop* and *Translucence* (cowritten with Samar Abdel Jaber) and the chapbooks *A Study in Spring* (cowritten with Zoe Ryder White), *The Deeply Flawed Human, Downtown*, and *Aging*. Her novella *The Couples* was published in 2019.

BRENDA CÁRDENAS is the author of *Boomerang* and the chapbooks *Bread of the Earth/The Last Colors*, with Roberto Harrison; *Achiote Seeds/Semillas de Achiote*, with Cristina García, Emmy Pérez, and Gabriela Erandi Rico; and *From the Tongues of Brick and Stone*. Cárdenas served as the Milwaukee Poet Laureate from 2010 to 2012 and teaches in the Creative Writing Program at the University of Wisconsin-Milwaukee.

YVONNE CASSIDY is the author of four novels: *The Other Boy, What Might Have Been Me, How Many Letters Are in Goodbye?*, and *I'm Right Here. How Many Letters Are in Goodbye?* was selected for the American Library Association's Rainbow Book List in 2017. She teaches at the Irish Arts Center and the Jewish Community Center in Manhattan.

CATHLEEN CHAMBLESS is a poet, a visual artist, and an activist. Her work has appeared in *The Electronic Encyclopedia of Experimental Literature, Jai–Alai, Fjords Review, Grief Diaries, Storm Cycle 2014* and *2015,* and *Wussy Mag.* Her debut collection of poetry, *Nec(Romantic),* was a finalist for the Bisexual Book Awards in 2016.

JESSICA CUELLO is the author of *Pricking* and *Hunt.* She has been awarded the 2017 CNY Book Award (for *Pricking*), the 2016 Washington Prize (for *Hunt*), the New Letters Poetry Prize, a Saltonstall Fellowship, and, most recently, the New Ohio Review Poetry Prize. Her newest poems are forthcoming in *Copper Nickel, Cave Wall, Bat City Review, Pleiades,* and *Barrow Street.*

SILVIA CURBELO's latest collection of poems, *Falling Landscape,* is available from Anhinga Press. Other collections include *The Secret History of Water* and a chapbook, *Ambush,* winner of the Main Street Rag contest. Awards include poetry fellowships from the National Endowment for the Arts, the Florida Division of Cultural Affairs, the Cintas Foundation, and the Writer's Voice, as well as the Jessica Noble Maxwell Poetry Prize from *American Poetry Review.*

DEBRA DEAN is the best-selling author of four critically acclaimed books that have been published in twenty-one languages. Her debut novel, *The Madonnas of Leningrad,* was a *New York Times* Editors' Choice, a #1 Booksense Pick, a *Booklist* Top Ten Novel, and an American Library Association Notable Book of the Year. Her newest book is *Hidden Tapestry.*

RITA DOVE, recipient of the 1987 Pulitzer Prize in poetry for *Thomas and Beulah,* was the US Poet Laureate from 1993 to 1995. Author of numerous books, most recently *Sonata Mulattica* and *Collected Poems 1974–2004,* she also edited *The Penguin Anthology of Twentieth-Century American Poetry.* Her many honors include the 2011 National Medal of Arts from President Obama, the 1996 National Humanities Medal from President Clinton, and twenty-eight honorary doctorates. Rita Dove is the Commonwealth Professor of English at the University of Virginia; she also serves as the *New York Times Magazine*'s poetry editor.

DENISE DUHAMEL's most recent book of poetry is *Scald*. *Blowout* was a finalist for the National Book Critics Circle Award. Her other titles include *Ka-Ching!*, *Two and Two*, *Queen for a Day: Selected and New Poems*, *The Star-Spangled Banner*, and *Kinky*. She also has coauthored four collaborative books with Maureen Seaton, the most recent of which is *CAPRICE*. She and Julie Marie Wade coauthored *The Unrhymables: Collaborations in Prose*. She is a Distinguished University Professor in the MFA program at Florida International University in Miami.

IRIS JAMAHL DUNKLE was the 2017–2018 Poet Laureate of Sonoma County, California. *Interrupted Geographies* is her third collection of poetry. Her other books include *Gold Passage* and *There's a Ghost in This Machine of Air*. Her work has been published in numerous publications, including the *San Francisco Chronicle*, *Fence*, *CALYX*, *Catamaran*, *Poet's Market 2013*, *Women's Studies*, and *Chicago Quarterly Review*. Dunkle teaches at Napa Valley College and is the poetry director of the Napa Valley Writers' Conference.

BETH ANN FENNELLY, Poet Laureate of Mississippi, teaches in the MFA program at the University of Mississippi, where she was named Outstanding Teacher of the Year. She's won grants from the National Endowment for the Arts and United States Artists, and won a Fulbright to Brazil. Her work has won a Pushcart Prize and three times been included in the Best American Poetry Series. Fennelly has published three poetry books—*Open House*, *Tender Hooks*, and *Unmentionables*—and a book of nonfiction, *Great with Child*.

ANNIE FINCH's six books of poetry include *Eve*, *Calendars*, and *Spells: New and Selected Poems*. Her poetry has been performed at Carnegie Hall, installed in the Cathedral of St. John the Divine, and published in *Poetry*, the *New York Times*, and *The Penguin Book of Twentieth-Century American Poetry.* Due out soon are *The Poetry Witch Book of Spells* and the anthology *A Womb of Our Own: Poets and Writers on Abortion.*

VANESSA GARCIA's debut novel, *White Light,* was named one of the Best Books of 2015 by NPR and won an International Latino Book Award. Most recently she was a Sesame Street Writer's Room Fellow and is currently a WP Theater Lab fellow and professor of writing at the Savannah College of Art and Design.

TERRY GODBEY has published four poetry collections: *Hold Still,* finalist for the Main Street Rag Poetry Book Award; *Beauty Lessons,* winner of the Quercus Review Poetry Book Award; *Behind Every Door,* winner of the Slipstream Poetry Chapbook Contest; and *Flame.* A winner of the Rita Dove Award in Poetry, she has also published more than 150 poems in literary magazines, including *Rattle, Poet Lore, Dogwood, CALYX, Crab Creek Review,* and the *Florida Review.* She is a wildlife and nature photographer who wanders in the woods every chance she gets.

CATHERINE GONICK's poetry has appeared in literary magazines including *Notre Dame Review, Ginosko,* and the anthology *in plein air.* She was awarded the Ina Coolbrith Memorial Prize for Poetry and was a finalist in the National Ten-Minute Play Contest with the Actors Theatre of Louisville.

MIRIAM BIRD GREENBERG is the author of *In the Volcano's Mouth,* winner of the 2015 Agnes Lynch Starrett Prize, and the chapbooks *All night in the new country* and *Pact-Blood, Fever Grass.* She's held fellowships from the National Endowment for the Arts, the Poetry Foundation, and the Fine Arts Work Center in Provincetown, Massachusetts. She lives in the San Francisco Bay Area.

JENNIFER MICHAEL HECHT is a poet and historian. Her most recent book of poetry is *Who Said*; her second, *Funny,* won the Felix Pollak Prize in Poetry from the University of Wisconsin Press, and her first, *The Next Ancient World,* won the Poetry Society of America's Norma Farber First Book Award. Hecht's poetry appears in the *American Poetry Review*, the *New Yorker*, the *New York Times*, *Poetry*, the *New Republic*, and the *Kenyon Review*. Hecht's *The End of the Soul* won Phi Beta Kappa's 2004 Ralph Waldo Emerson Award in intellectual history. She is currently working on a book about poetry.

VICKI HENDRICKS is the author of the noir novels *Miami Purity*, *Iguana Love*, *Voluntary Madness*, *Sky Blues*, and *Cruel Poetry*, an Edgar Finalist in 2008. She recently retired from teaching at Broward College and moved to De Leon Springs in central Florida, the rural locale of her most recent novel, *Fur People*.

MICHAEL HETTICH has published over a dozen books and chapbooks of poetry, most recently *Bluer and More Vast: Prose Poems*. Other books include *The Frozen Harbor*, *Systems of Vanishing*, and *To Start an Orchard*. He has published widely in such journals as *Orion*, *Ploughshares*, *TriQuarterly*, *Prairie Schooner*, and *Poetry East*. He recently moved from Miami, Florida, to Black Mountain, North Carolina.

BRENDA HILLMAN is a poet, an educator, an editor, and an activist. She is the author of ten collections of poetry with Wesleyan University Press, most recently *Seasonal Works with Letters on Fire* and *Extra Hidden Life, among the Days*. She has coedited volumes by Richard O. Moore and with Patricia Dienstfrey, *The Grand Permission: New Writings on Poetics and Motherhood*. Hillman recently co-translated *At Your Feet*, the poems of Ana Cristina Cesar. She serves as the Filippi Professor of Poetry at Saint Mary's College of California.

LAURA LEE HUTTENBACH is the author of two books: *The Boy Is Gone* and *Running with Raven*. In 2016, she moved to New York City as a graduate student and Chair's Fellow at New York University's Arthur L. Carter Journalism Institute.

BOSCH JONES is a poet, an artist, and a performer residing in South Florida. His poems have appeared in the *Paris Review*, *La Presa*, *IMPACT*, and *Blood and Tears: A Collection of Poems for Matthew Shepard*, among others.

JEN KARETNICK is the author of three full-length poetry collections, including *The Treasures That Prevail,* finalist for the 2017 Poetry Society of Virginia Book Prize, and four poetry chapbooks. She is the winner of the 2017 Hart Crane Memorial Poetry Contest, the 2016 Romeo Lemay Poetry Prize, and the 2015 Anna Davidson Rosenberg Prize. She is the cofounder and coeditor of the daily online literary journal *SWWIM Every Day.*

GERRY LAFEMINA's latest book is the poetry collection *The Story of Ash.* He is also the author of *The Parakeets of Brooklyn, Notes for the Novice Ventriloquist* (prose poems), *Vanishing Horizon,* and *Little Heretic.* The former director of the Frostburg Center for Literary Arts, he teaches at Frostburg State University and serves as a mentor in the MFA program at Carlow University.

LUCIA LEAO is a full-time translator and writer. She has published a collection of short stories and is the coauthor of a young adult novel, both published in Portuguese in Brazil. She was born in Rio de Janeiro.

MIA LEONIN is the author of four poetry collections—*Fable of the Pack-Saddle Child, Braid, Unraveling the Bed,* and *Chance Born*—and a memoir, *Havana and Other Missing Fathers.* Leonin has been awarded fellowships from the State of Florida Department of Cultural Affairs for her poetry and creative nonfiction, as well as two Money for Women grants by the Barbara Deming Fund, and she has been a fellow at the USC Annenberg/National Endowment for the Arts Journalism Institute in Theater and Musical Theater. She teaches creative writing at the University of Miami in Coral Gables, Florida.

GAIL CARSON LEVINE's first poetry collection for adults, *Transient,* came out in 2016. Her poems have appeared in the *Louisville Review,* the *Sugar House Review,* the *Lullwater Review, The Golden Shovel Anthology: New Poems Honoring Gwendolyn Brooks,* and others. She's best known for her books for children, in particular *Ella Enchanted.*

KYLE CARRERO LOPEZ is the recipient of a Goldwater Fellowship and a Global Research Initiative Fellowship to Berlin, from New York University, and a TuCuba Fellowship from the CubaOne Foundation. He has poems published or forthcoming in *Poetry*, the *Cincinnati Review*, the *Florida Review*, and elsewhere.

TRISH MACENULTY is the author of *The Pink House, Wait Until Tomorrow: A Daughter's Memoir*, and several other books. Most recently, she edited *Howl, 2016*, an anthology of poems, essays, and rants.

RITA MARIA MARTINEZ is the author of the poetry collection *The Jane and Bertha in Me*, inspired by Charlotte Brontë's fiery governess and infamous madwoman. Her work has been nominated for a Pushcart Prize and has appeared in publications such as the *Notre Dame Review, Ploughshares*, and *The Best American Poetry Blog*. Martinez lives in Florida.

CAITLIN GRACE MCDONNELL was a New York Times Fellow in poetry at New York University and has received fellowships from Yaddo, Blue Mountain Center, and the Fine Arts Work Center in Provincetown. Her poems and essays have been published widely, and she published a chapbook of poems, *Dreaming the Tree*, and a collection, *Looking for Small Animals*. Currently, she teaches English at City University of New York, lives in Brooklyn with her daughter, and is at work on a novel.

FREESIA MCKEE is author of the chapbook *How Distant the City*. Her words have appeared in *cream city review, The Feminist Wire, HuffPost*, and the *Ms. Magazine Blog*, among other publications. Her book reviews have appeared in *South Florida Poetry Journal, Gulf Stream*, and the *Drunken Odyssey*. Freesia is the winner of *Cut-Bank Literary Magazine*'s 2018 Patricia Goedicke Prize in Poetry.

M. B. MCLATCHEY is the recipient of the American Poet Prize from the *American Poetry Journal* and the 2013 May Swenson Award for her debut poetry collection, *The Lame God*. Currently serving as the Florida Poet Laureate for Volusia County, she is a professor of classics at Embry-Riddle Aeronautical University in Daytona, Florida.

DAVID MCLOGHLIN is the author of *Waiting for Saint Brendan and Other Poems*, *Santiago Sketches*, and *Crash Centre* (forthcoming). *Sign Tongue*, his rendering of the work of the Chilean poet Enrique Winter, won the 2014 Goodmorning Menagerie Chapbook-in-Translation prize. He is a Pushcart Prize nominee, and his work has been published in journals such as *Poetry Ireland Review*, *Barrow Street*, *The Moth*, and *Poetry International*, and has been broadcast on WNYC's *Radiolab*.

ANA MENÉNDEZ has published four books of fiction: *Adios, Happy Homeland!*, *The Last War*, *Loving Che*, and *In Cuba I Was a German Shepherd*, whose title story won a Pushcart Prize. Her work has appeared in a variety of publications, including *Vogue*, *Bomb*, the *New York Times*, and *Tin House*, and has been included in several anthologies, including *The Norton Anthology of Latino Literature*. A former Fulbright Scholar in Egypt, she is now a program director with Academic Affairs at Florida International University.

HOLLY MITCHELL is the winner of the 2017 Amy Award from *Poets & Writers* and a 2012 Gertrude Claytor Prize from the Academy of American Poets. Her poems have been included in *Circe's Lament: Anthology of Wild Women* and have appeared in several journals, including the *Baltimore Review*, *Day One*, *Juked*, *Narrative Magazine*, and *Paperbag*.

JENNY MOLBERG is the author of *Marvels of the Invisible* (winner of the 2014 Berkshire Prize, Tupelo Press, 2017) and *Refusal* (2020). She is the recipient of a Creative Writing Fellowship from the National Endowment for the Arts, as well as fellowships from the Sewanee Writers Conference, Vermont Studio Center, and C. D. Wright Women Writers Conference. She teaches creative writing at the University of Central Missouri, where she directs Pleiades Press and edits *Pleiades* magazine.

CATHERINE MOORE is the author of three chapbooks and the poetry book *ULLA! ULLA!* Her work appears in *Tahoma Literary Review*, *Southampton Review*, *Mid-American Review*, *Broad River Review*, and various anthologies. She's been awarded Walker Percy and Hambidge Fellowships, the *Southeast Review*'s Gearhart Poetry Prize 2014, a Pushcart Prize, Best of the Net, and VERA Award nominations.

DAVID MOSCOVICH is the Romanian American author of *You Are Make Very Important Bathtime* and *LIFE+70[Redacted]*, a print version of the single most expensive literary e-book ever to be hacked. His latest novel is *Blink If You Love Me*. He lives in New York and Porto, Portugal.

EILEEN MYLES is the recipient of a Guggenheim Fellowship, an Andy Warhol/Creative Capital Arts Writers Grant, four Lambda Book Awards, the Shelley Prize from the Poetry Society of America, and a poetry award from the Foundation for Contemporary Arts. In 2016, they received a Creative Capital grant and the Clark Prize for Excellence in Art Writing. They live in New York and Marfa, Texas.

CYNTHIA NEELY is the winner of Bright Hill Press's chapbook contest for *Passing Through Blue Earth* and the winner of *Flyway: Journal of Writing and Environment*'s chapbook contest for *Broken Water*. Her poems, essays, and creative nonfiction have appeared in numerous journals, including *Pontoon*, *Bellevue Literary Review*, and *Crab Creek Review*, and in several anthologies. Her book *Flight Path* was a finalist in the Aldrich Press book contest. Neely earned her MFA in creative writing from Pacific University.

RHONDA J. NELSON's books include *Musical Chair* and *The Undertow*. She is a Florida Fellow in Poetry 2000–2001, the winner of Writer's Exchange 2000, and the recipient of two Hillsborough County Emerging Artist grants and one Hillsborough County Individual Artist Grant. Her work has been published in many journals, including *Ekphrasis*, *Angel Face*, *Slipstream*, *The Panhandler*,

Survivor Magazine, Asheville Review, Apalachee Review, and *Sandhill Review*. She is *Creative Loafing* magazine's Best Spoken Word Artist 2019.

BARBRA NIGHTINGALE's poems have appeared in numerous poetry journals and anthologies, including *Rattle*, the *Florida Review*, *Barrow Street*, and elsewhere. Her newest book is *Alphalexia*. She's an associate editor with the *South Florida Poetry Review* and a professor emeritus from Broward College.

MICHAEL MACKIN O'MARA, born in Brooklyn, New York, lives in West Palm Beach, Florida, where he works at a nonprofit. He is *SoFloPoJo*'s (*South Florida Poetry Journal*) managing editor and co-publisher, and has recent work in *fields magazine*, the *Schuylkill Valley Journal, Chantwood Magazine, Slag Review, The Body, The Complete HIV/AIDS Resource*, and *Switched-On Gutenberg*.

MOLLY PEACOCK is a widely anthologized poet, as well as a biographer. Her latest poetry collections are *The Analyst* and *Cornucopia: New and Selected Poems*. She is the cofounder of Poetry in Motion on New York's subways and buses and the series founder of The Best Canadian Poetry. One of the subjects of a documentary about women who choose not to have children, *My So-Called Selfish Life*, she is also the author of the biography *The Paper Garden: Mrs. Delany Begins Her Life's Work at 72*.

MARGE PIERCY has published nineteen books of poetry, including *The Moon Is Always Female, The Crooked Inheritance, The Hunger Moon: Selected Poems*, and *Made in Detroit*. Her seventeen novels include *Woman on the Edge of Time; Gone to Soldiers; He, She and It*; and *Sex Wars*. Her memoir is *Sleeping with Cats*. She has published four nonfiction books, including *Pesach for the Rest of Us* and, with Ira Wood, *So You Want to Write*. Every year she holds a juried intensive poetry workshop in Wellfleet, Massachusetts.

CATHERINE ESPOSITO PRESCOTT is the author of the chapbooks *Maria Sings* and *The Living Ruin*. Recent poems have appeared in *Bellevue Literary Review, Flyway, MiPOesias, Pleiades*, and *Po-*

etry East, as well as the anthologies *99 Poets for the 99 Percent* and *The Orison Anthology*. Prescott is a cofounder of SWWIM, which curates a reading series in Miami Beach and publishes the online literary journal *SWWIM Every Day*.

ALEXANDRA LYTTON REGALADO's poetry collection *Matria* is the winner of the St. Lawrence Book Award. Her work has appeared in *The Best American Poetry 2018*, *Narrative*, *Gulf Coast*, the *Notre Dame Review*, and *Creative Nonfiction*, among others. Cofounder of Kalina Press, Regalado is the author, editor, and/or translator of more than ten Central America–themed books, including *Vanishing Points: Contemporary Salvadoran Prose*. She is the winner of the 2015 Coniston Poetry Prize and the recipient of a Letras Latinas/ PINTURA PALABRA DC Ekphrastic residency. Her ongoing photo-essay project about El Salvador, through_the_bulletproof_ glass, is on Instagram.

SAPPHIRE became involved in the slam poetry movement, writing, performing, and eventually publishing her work after moving to New York in the late 1970s from California, where she was born. She is the author of two collections of poetry, *Black Wings & Blind Angels* and *American Dreams*, and of the *New York Times* best-selling novels *The Kid* and *Push*, which was made into the Academy Award–winning movie *Precious*. She has performed her work in venues in North America, Europe, Africa, and South America.

MAUREEN SEATON has authored numerous poetry collections, both solo and collaborative, most recently, *Sweet World* and *Fisher*. Her awards include the Iowa Prize, the Lambda Literary Award, the Audre Lorde Award, a National Endowment for the Arts Fellowship, and the Pushcart. Her memoir, *Sex Talks to Girls*, also garnered a Lambda Literary Award. With poet Neil de la Flor, she edited the anthology *Reading Queer: Poetry in a Time of Chaos*. Seaton teaches creative writing at the University of Miami.

MAGGIE SMITH is the author of the prizewinning books *Lamp of the Body* and *The Well Speaks of Its Own Poison*. Smith has received a Pushcart Prize, as well as fellowships and awards from the National Endowment for the Arts, the Sustainable Arts Foundation, the Ohio Arts Council, and the Academy of American Poets. Her work has appeared in the *New York Times, Tin House, APR, The Believer,* the *Paris Review,* the *Kenyon Review, Ploughshares, Best American Poetry,* and on the CBS prime-time drama *Madam Secretary.*

CHRISTOPHER SOTO is the author of the chapbook *Sad Girl Poems* and the editor of *Nepantla: An Anthology Dedicated to Queer Poets of Color.* He cofounded the Undocupoets Campaign and worked with Amazon Literary Partnerships to establish grants for undocumented writers. In 2017 he was awarded the Freedom Plow Award for Poetry & Activism by Split This Rock, and he was invited to teach a Poetry and Protest Movements course at Columbia University, as part of the June Jordan Teaching Corp. In 2016 *Poets & Writers* honored Christopher Soto with the Barnes & Noble Writer for Writers Award.

VIRGIL SUÁREZ was born in Havana, Cuba, in 1962. He is the author of four novels, two memoirs, two collections of stories, and eight volumes of poetry, most recently *90 Miles: Selected and New.* Currently he is putting the finishing touches on his new book of poems, *The Painted Bunting's Last Molt.* When he is not writing, he is riding his Yamaha V-Star 1100 Classic Motorcycle up and down the Blue Highways of the South. He lives with his wife in Florida.

KELLY SUNDBERG's debut memoir, *Goodbye, Sweet Girl: A Story of Domestic Violence and Survival,* was released in 2018. Her essays have appeared or are forthcoming in *Alaska Quarterly Review, Guernica, Slice Magazine, Gulf Coast, Denver Quarterly,* and elsewhere. She has been the recipient of fellowships or grants from the Vermont Studio Center, Dickinson House, A Room of Her Own Foundation, and the National Endowment for the Arts.

COLLEEN SUTTON writes creative nonfiction, short fiction, and poetry, and is currently working on her first novel. A diplomat for the Government of Canada by day, Colleen's also a certified yoga instructor, lifeguard, and professional dog trainer.

PAUL TRAN is the recipient of the Ruth Lilly and Dorothy Sargent Rosenberg Fellowship from *Poetry* magazine and the Discovery/ *Boston Review* Poetry Prize. Their work appears in the *New Yorker*, *Poetry*, and elsewhere, including the anthology *Inheriting the War* and the movie *Love Beats Rhymes*. Paul is the first Asian American since 1993 to win the Nuyorican Poets Cafe Grand Slam. They serve as poetry editor at *The Offing* magazine and Chancellor's Graduate Fellow in the Writing Program at Washington University in St. Louis.

EMMA TRELLES is the author of *Tropicalia*, winner of the Andrés Montoya Poetry Prize, a finalist for Foreword INDIES poetry book of the year, and a recommended read by *The Rumpus*. She is currently writing a second book of poems, *Courage and the Clock*. Her work has been anthologized in *Best American Poetry*, *Best of the Net*, *Verse Daily*, and elsewhere. Recent poems appear in the *Colorado Review*, *Spillway*, the *Miami Rail*, *Zócalo Public Square*, and *SWWIM*. A recipient of an Individual Artist Fellowship from the Florida Division of Cultural Affairs and a founding member of the AWP Latinx Caucus, she lives with her husband in California, where she teaches at Santa Barbara City College and programs the Mission Poetry Series.

JULIE MARIE WADE is the author of ten collections of poetry and prose, including *Wishbone: A Memoir in Fractures*, *Small Fires*, *Postage Due*, *When I Was Straight*, *SIX*, and *Same-Sexy Marriage: A Novella in Poems*. With Denise Duhamel, she wrote *The Unrhymables: Collaborations in Prose*. A recipient of the Lambda Literary Award for Lesbian Memoir and grants from the Kentucky Arts Council and the Barbara Deming Memorial Fund, Wade teaches in the creative writing program at Florida International University and reviews regularly for *Lambda Literary Review* and *The Rumpus*. She is married to Angie Griffin and lives on Hollywood Beach.

ZOE WELCH is a photo-based artist and writer. Her written work and hybrid visual poetry have appeared in publications in French and English in Canada, and her public art has been showcased in Seattle and Miami. In her current work, Zoe is exploring what it means to live in America, where she moved in 2016.

CYNTHIA WHITE's poems have appeared or are forthcoming in *Narrative*, *Grist*, *New Letters*, *Poet Lore*, and *ZYZZYVA*, among others. She was a finalist for Nimrod's Pablo Neruda Prize and the winner of the Julia Darling Memorial Prize for Poetry from Kallisto Gaia Press. She lives in Santa Cruz, California.

JAVIER ZAMORA was born in El Salvador and migrated to the US when he was nine. He is a Radcliffe Institute Fellow at Harvard and holds fellowships from CantoMundo, Colgate University, the Lannan Foundation, MacDowell, the National Endowment for the Arts, the Poetry Foundation, Stanford University, and Yaddo. Zamora's poems appear in *Granta*, the *Kenyon Review*, *Poetry*, the *New York Times*, and elsewhere. *Unaccompanied* is his first collection.

HARI ZIYAD is a New York–based storyteller, the author of *Black Boy Out of Time: A Never Coming of Age Story*, and the editor in chief of *RaceBaitR*. They are also a script consultant on the untitled Tarell McCraney television series coming to OWN, the managing editor of Black Youth Project, and an assistant editor for *Vinyl Poetry & Prose*.

CREDITS

The editors gratefully acknowledge the following publications in which contributor works have previously appeared:

"Because What We Do Does Not Die," from *Indigo*. Originally published in *Narrative* (2019). Copyright © 2019, 2020 by Ellen Bass. Reprinted with the permission of the Permissions Company, LLC, on behalf of Copper Canyon Press, www.coppercanyonpress.org. "The Pallor of Survival," from *The Hour Between Dog and Wolf*. Copyright © 1997 by Laure-Anne Bosselaar. Reprinted with the permission of the Permissions Company, LLC, on behalf of BOA Editions, Ltd., www.boaeditions.org. "Layover" and "Duplex," by Jericho Brown, reprinted from *The Tradition* (Copper Canyon Press, 2019). Fred Courtright, the Permissions Company, LLC, rights agency for Copper Canyon Press. "me too," by Nicole Callihan, first appeared in *Rise Up Review* (2018). "For a Minute There, I Thought We Could've Been Happy," by Cathleen Chambless, first appeared in *Nec(Romantic)* (Gorilla Press, 2016). "The Peach Orchard," by Rita Dove, first appeared in *Meridian* 2 (Fall 1998). "It's Just Words, Folks, It's Just Words," by Denise Duhamel, first appeared in *Resist Much/Obey Little: Inaugural Poems to the Resistance* (Spuyten Duyvil Press, 2017). "Questionnaire for Two Pussies," by Denise Duhamel and Maureen Seaton, first appeared in the *South Carolina Review* (Fall 2017). "Threshold," by Denise Duhamel and Julie Marie Wade, first appeared in *No Tokens* 2 (Fall 2014). "Daughter, They'll Use Even Your Own Gaze to Wound You," by Beth Ann Fennelly, first appeared in *Heating & Cooling: 52 Micro-Memoirs* (W. W. Norton, 2017). "The Root," by Annie Finch, first appeared in *Poetry* (March 2019). "Sweet Sixteen," by Terry Godbey, first appeared in *Slipstream* (2009). "Cocoa Beach," by Terry Godbey, first appeared in *Passager* (2012). "Killing," by Miriam Bird Greenberg, from *In the Volcano's Mouth* © 2016. Reprinted with the permission of the University of Pittsburgh Press. "Gender Bender," by Jennifer Michael Hecht, first appeared in the *New Yorker* (2011). "Me Too Limerick with Six Drumbeats," by Brenda Hillman, first appeared in the *Gambler* (2016). "Learning," by Gail Carson Levine, originally appeared in *Transient* (Nightshade Press, an imprint of Keystone College Press, 2016). "Date Grape," by Freesia McKee, first appeared in *The Feminist Wire* (2017). "Bingo Night for Missing and Exploited Children," by M. B. McLatchy, first appeared in *The Lame God* (Utah State University Press, 2013). "One in Four," by David McLoghlin, first appeared in *Waiting for Saint Brendan and Other Poems* (Salmon Poetry, 2012). "Epistle from the Hospital for Harassment," by Jenny Molberg, first appeared in the *Journal* (Winter 2018). "Said the Poet,"